The Gated Society

Exploring Information Age Realities for Schools

Everette Surgenor

Published in partnership with the
American Association of School Administrators

ROWMAN & LITTLEFIELD EDUCATION
Lanham • *New York* • *Toronto* • *Plymouth, UK*

Published in partnership with
the American Association of School Administrators

Published in the United States of America
by Rowman & Littlefield Education
A division of Rowman & Littlefield Publishers, Inc.
A wholly owned subsidiary of The Rowman & Littlefield Publishing Group, Inc.
4501 Forbes Boulevard, Suite 200, Lanham, Maryland 20706
www.rowmaneducation.com

Estover Road
Plymouth PL6 7PY
United Kingdom

British Library Cataloguing in Publication Information Available

Library of Congress Cataloging-in-Publication Data

Surgenor, E. W.
 The gated society : exploring information age realities for schools / Everette Surgenor.
  p. cm.
 ISBN-13: 978-1-57886-931-2 (cloth : alk. paper)
 ISBN-10: 1-57886-931-5 (cloth : alk. paper)
 ISBN-13: 978-1-57886-932-9 (pbk. : alk. paper)
 ISBN-10: 1-57886-932-3 (pbk. : alk. paper)
 ISBN-13: 978-1-57886-933-6 (electronic)
 ISBN-10: 1-57886-933-1 (electronic)
 1. Public schools—United States. 2. Public schools—Canada. 3. Educational
change—United States. 4. Educational change—Canada. 5. School improvement
programs—United States. 6. School improvement programs—Canada. I. Title.
 LA217.2.S874 2009
 371.010973—dc22   2008030585

My deep appreciation and thanks for Denny Kemprud and Lach Farrell for their advice and feedback, to my brother Neil for his insight and observations and to my wife Lavern for her support, help, and encouragement over the eight years it has taken to bring this book to fruition.

Contents

Introduction

Thirty years after becoming qualified to teach, I retired from public education. I enjoyed a broad range of experiences as an educator and had many moments that were personally and professionally satisfying. I taught a variety of grade levels and subjects and was the principal of five different schools ranging from a two-room rural elementary school to a grade eight through twelve secondary school. I was also the superintendent in four districts over a fifteen-year period.

During my career I was fortunate to work in partnership with many other professionals on exciting initiatives. They included the:

• use of technology for communications and learning purposes;
• creation of a provincial telecommunications network for education;
• reform of secondary education;
• advancement of technology and trades in schools;
• creation of pathways between grade twelve and first year college; and
• service on a rural task force challenged to investigate and report on the state of rural education in the Province of British Columbia (Canada).

These initiatives allowed me to meet with, and learn from, many educators across the United States and Canada.

Yet, when I retired, I did so with a sense of dissatisfaction and a deep frustration. The public education system was on a pathway toward becoming more political in its decision making and less relevant to those who needed its services. I feared that there was no unified will or desire at any level to begin doing what needed to be done in terms of initiating some very necessary reforms.

There have been attempts to bring about change over the past few decades. There have been some changes, but the public education system has the capacity to slowly and quietly resist all attempts at systemic change or reform. The *core system* I retired from was basically the same one I entered as a learner some fifty-plus years earlier. Its DNA remains unchanged. As the Chinese proverb says, "If we don't change our direction we're likely to end up where we're headed."[1]

The resistance to change has become even more tangible and definable over the past fifteen years. The balance of power within the education system has shifted during this time period. It now caters more to the people delivering the service than to those needing or receiving the service.

The impetus for selecting *The Gated Society* as a title came from reading a series of press releases issued by U.S. governors in January 2005. These releases expressed serious concerns about declining levels of student achievement in the United States. Bill Gates, who was acting as an advisor to the governors, connected these declines to his belief that secondary schools were "obsolete."

During the late 1980s and early 1990s many professionals within education served the same notice and made attempts to change the system. They developed many exciting initiatives designed to bring about change but they did not succeed. Chief among the reasons for failure was the resistance by special interest groups within education as well as by political, community, and business leaders. The reasons for this resistance are discussed in later chapters.

Now, twenty years later, these political and business leaders complain that the system is not working. They come forward with proposals to raise standards and create more rigor as a means of addressing the systemwide problems. By doing so, they ignore history and completely miss the point about initiating change.

The Gated Society is a metaphor for a North American culture that is guided by industrial age assumptions, mindsets, and models. It is a culture that continues to create change for the future by constantly reinventing the past. It is also a culture enamored of, and trapped by, its past success. Reform initiatives, like the ones proposed by the governors, fail because they are structured around industrial age understandings of change and reform. They haven't, can't, and won't work.

The title is also a reference to the power and influence that leaders like Bill Gates and others exercise within our society. It is a model of power and leadership that has a negative impact on the society. It is a model driven by corporate, political, and financial needs, but it does not focus on nation-building, sustaining democracy, and maintaining a quality way of life for all citizens. It appears that the culture perpetuated by this model is prepared to write off a whole generation of young people. There is no doubt that Mr. Gates has contributed a lot of resources to help the less fortunate around the globe. But the business community he represents seems to have little interest in the major issues that face North American society. The financial success and the influence of that community continue to be built around past practice. It has little to do with creating a positive and equitable future for all citizens. These corporate leaders have the ear of governments and they influence policies that are quite self-serving. Their claims about being on the cutting edge of change and about being world leaders in the introduction of information age thinking and practice are mostly a myth. The leadership for the type of change envisioned in this book is not to be found within their ranks.

The third title reference, and perhaps the most troubling, is recognition that we are a society held together, yet divided, by those things that make us different. Being different can be a powerful force within the culture if it is used to enrich the collective experience. But when it is used to keep us apart, we then have the seeds of discontent and disorder waiting for the opportunity to grow.

Gated communities, for example, are common all across North America. Their existence sometimes speaks to people's fears or suspicions about other groups in the society. They also represent economic, social, religious, ethnic, and sometimes political, divisions in our communities. These *gated communities* are individually, and sometimes collectively, ones of choice, of commonality, of affluence, of purpose, and of religion and/or belief. They are usually exclusionary. Other gated communities exist that are determined more by unfavorable economic and social circumstances. In these communities, location is not always a choice. The *gates* of poverty, unemployment, and race are not as visible but are just as real. One set of gates swings open to opportunity and influence while the other closes access to the same.

This book identifies the intellectual, emotional, and organizational factors that keep us locked within the industrial age paradigm. These factors are preventing and inhibiting the societal shift to the paradigm of the information age. The exploration of these factors creates understanding and awareness about the *what* and *why* of change we are currently facing. Some processes are proposed that can be used to begin a systemic change initiative designed to benefit the whole of society and not just specific individuals or interest groups within it.

This book is critical of existing practice and, sometimes, of practitioners. These comments are often phrased in very specific language with the intent to promote and provoke reflection and discussion. At times there is a tendency toward generalizations, but the views and opinions expressed are based on personal observations and experiences.

The motivation for writing this book is to initiate a discussion that will lead to the creation of a competent and relevant public education system that will continue to be a linchpin for democratic processes in our society; processes that enable equity of access and opportunity for all citizens.

There is a significant emphasis on learning, and how people learn, within the structure of this book. That is because the research on learning provides essential understanding and insights about the nature of the reforms for the practice, form, and function of our education systems. The research also provides insight to the changes that other organizations and institutions within our society need to make. That is, if they wish to be sustainable and competitive in a knowledge-based society and economy.

In order to make these changes, all of us must be prepared to open the gates that hinder our progress and begin the journey into a new reality. Like early explorers, we have no maps that show us where to go or how to get there. It is not a journey for the weak, the cautious, the uninformed, or those who have the most to benefit by staying at home and keeping the gates closed.

People in other parts of the world, unencumbered by an industrial age past and living in societies with great divisions between those who *have* and those who *have not,* are hungry for change and have little concern about the impact of that change upon North American society. Nor should they.

They are ambitious and driven. We are complacent and compliant. They live in societies without political opposition and are able to direct and redirect resources and people as they see fit to accomplish their goals. We are at a disadvantage because we have no common reference point for change. Ours is a fragmented society whereby people use democratic processes to protect their special interests or lobbies. The concept of the greater good for all is not central to the thinking of political, social, and economic decision makers.

These observations are by no means an endorsement for autocratic rule, but it does point out how complex and challenging the change process can be in a democratic society.

This book is not an academic work. It is based upon my perceptions, reflections, learning, and experiences over the past two decades. The differences between the industrial age and information age paradigms are explored and suggestions are made as to how those differences might impact on the practice, form, and function of education systems.

To do this requires a commitment from a vast majority of us to change. We need to *get in the game.* Our collective futures are dependent on it, both for ourselves and for our children and grandchildren. As Franklin Roosevelt said in his speech to the Democratic National Convention, "To some generations, much is given. Of other generations much is expected."[2] I come from a generation to whom much has been given. This book is an effort to give something back.

NOTES

1. Chinese proverb, Quotations Page, www.quotationspage.com/search.php3? homesearch=If+we+don%27t+change&startsearch=Search.
2. Franklin D. Roosevelt, Speech to the Democratic National Convention (June 27, 1936), Wikiquote, en.wikiquote.org/wiki/Franklin_D._Roosevelt#Speech_to_the_ Democratic_National_Convention_.281936.29.

Chapter One

Learning in an Age of New Realities

To create something you must be something.[1]

Being impervious to change is not a harbinger of good things to come for the public education system, especially when globalism has impacted the nature and substance of almost every other organization and institution in our society. This insight alone should be enough to alert the public to the challenges facing public education systems across North America. But it hasn't, and therein lies the problem.

The need for change was better understood and supported at many different levels during the late 1980s and early 1990s. But even with that understanding and initial support, attempts at creating significant change eventually failed.

These efforts were not wrong; they were just poorly conceived. The innovators and their political partners did not understand the nature and structure of the evolving paradigm called the information age. The attempted innovations, although well intended, were never successful because they were anchored in industrial age thinking and practice. Instead of trying to transform the existing education system they should have being trying to transcend it.

The people with the most to lose by these change initiatives soon went on the attack. They described the reform efforts as uninformed experiments and suggested that children's futures were at risk because of them. Parents became nervous, and politicians jumped into the fray. They were quietly influenced by the lobbies of special interest and motivated by the opportunity to make political gain on people's fears. The politicians referenced what they knew best and what had served them well—their past. They opted for stability rather than risk the turmoil associated with exploring the unknown.

7

The forces of the status quo halted the reform attempts because those initiating the reforms lacked the knowledge, skill, and understanding to explain the new paradigm and to structure their reforms with it. Consequently educators were soon dealing with the mindless and numbing rhetoric about standards, accountability, and *back to the basics*.

Instead of looking forward they began a journey that led us back to our past. Sadly, education systems have wasted fifteen years or more ignoring reality. They have become consumed by initiatives about standards and basics that are not relevant to the future needs of learners. Political and professional leaders, steeped in the past, with power in the present, have compromised the future.

Valuable time has been lost in addressing the problems that beset the education system. This is due to the collective ignorance and self-interest of our society.

North Americans are woefully uninformed about the trends and realities of the twenty-first century. Many other parts of the world understand them, or at least acknowledge their existence, and are making efforts to try *adapt and adopt* within their societies. They are anxious to be part of the future and not just passive eyewitnesses to the evolution of the information age. Because we have restrained *what might be*, we are in danger of becoming chained to *what was*.

Our past success and past achievements have left us so sedated that we are unaware that the rules that govern success have changed. There are individuals and groups within our society who recognize what is happening, but that recognition is not systemic nor is it stimulating the types of societal change that we need. Our circumstances are akin to the smoker who, knowing that smoking will shorten his or her life, continues to sustain the habit, day in and day out, despite the threat of death.

The challenge is to create and foster awareness about these circumstances and link them to a set of likely consequences. This will spark conversation and generate action about what needs to change or be reformed. Some responses might take the form of anger or vindictiveness because many people will be hearing or understanding the issues for the first time. But something needs to happen to shock people out of their passivity so that they can fulfill their responsibility as citizens in a democratic society.

It is highly unlikely that any individual or group can initiate action on their own. Certainly teachers and principals have no mandate to make the type of changes envisioned in this book. Neither do boards, superintendents, schools, or districts. It is a collective responsibility resting equally with parents, politicians, business and community leaders, as well as members of the public education system. Educators are part of the problem, but they are also integral to the solution. The ownership of change cannot be made to rest solely in their hands.

The change process should not be based on an assumption that everything we presently have or do in public education is wrong and needs to be changed. It isn't. But there must be a process to validate and sustain what is the best of present practice as well as a process to stop doing what no longer makes sense. In order to do this we must first establish a new context for education and then validate what we keep and what we don't within the framework of that context.

This book is not about the failure of schools, but about the nature of that failure. Certainly it could be argued that the education system is not failing if we use the model by which most of us received our formal education as a reference point. But if the reference point is the type of education all learners need to be successful in work, learning, or as a citizen in the twenty-first century, then the case for change is clear.

These points of reference perspectives raise two fundamentally different issues. One has to do with sustaining an educational model that perpetuates our industrial age past while the other has to do with creating an educational model that allows us to fully participate in an information age—present and future.

Our past experience with change initiatives should be enough to convince most observers that the industrial age model of education cannot be adapted, modified, transformed, or changed to serve the needs of the information age society. This is true of all industrial age organizations. The two paradigms are incompatible and not interchangeable. The new paradigm operates differently and demands new ways of thinking, working, and organizing. We need to transcend the existing system and not waste any more resources and effort on trying to transform it.

One has only to read the newspapers, listen to the radio, or watch news programs to understand how widespread the perception is that public education systems are failing. There are numerous articles and commentaries about this failure usually based on assessment reports that reveal low student performance and achievement. Unfortunately, the stated reasons for these results are usually followed by politically motivated solutions that have more to do with instituting past practice than they do about creating new ones. Their solutions are intuitive, clear, concise, and wrong.

Consider recent comments at the National Education Summit on High Schools held by the National Governors Association and Achieve, Inc. in Washington, D.C. Bill Gates spoke at this gathering and said: "America's high schools are obsolete. By obsolete, I don't just mean that our high schools are broken, flawed and under funded—though a case could be made for every one of those points. By obsolete, I mean that our high schools—even when they're working exactly as designed—cannot teach our kids what they need to know today."[2]

The governors convened a meeting on the state of education because they were alarmed at the number of secondary students in the United States who were failing. Their proposed solutions for addressing the problem referred back to what they knew and understood about their educational experience. They called for more rigors in high school courses, higher standards, and a better alignment between graduation requirements and the skills demanded in college or work. They seemed to completely ignore the comment by Bill Gates that secondary schools cannot teach our kids what they need to know today. The governors' proposed solutions in no way acknowledged that insight.

Neither did their proposed solutions make any reference to the research on learning and how people learn. Nor were there any comments about the need for systemic organizational change or reform. The people trying to create change were seeking political solutions and were constrained in doing so by their lack of knowledge and understanding of the problem.

This is an example of industrial age thinking at its best. Bill Gates clearly identified the problem in his summary comments, but both he and the governors missed the solution. Or maybe they recognized that the political environment that is needed to create the necessary changes is not there, and that it is better in terms of public relations to give a sense of trying to do something than do nothing at all.

This is hinted at in one comment at the conclusion of his speech when Mr. Gates indicated that amassing the political will to make the necessary change was the greatest obstacle to making the changes.

The reality is that these types of political prognostications tend to fall upon deaf ears. They generate no meaningful reform or initiate any change process within our communities. Members of the public, and educators, have heard these types of comments too many times. They are insulated from the message and seemingly incapable of action, even though there seems to be a general recognition that the education system is broken and can't be fixed.

When the blame is assigned for what is wrong within the system, much of it seems to fall, paradoxically, at the feet of the learner. Low achievement results, high drop-out rates, and low skill acquisition are often attributed to a lack of effort or a lack of interest on the part of the student. Failure in schools, and of schools, is directly attributed to low literacy levels, a negative attitude, a poor neighborhood, bad nutritional habits, the increase of single-parent families, a lack of standards, cultural diversity, and so on.

All of these items, individually or collectively, might be contributing factors to creating a more challenging learning environment, but the problem for achievement and success rests elsewhere. It rests in the process for training teachers, curriculum models in use, classroom practice, instructional methodology, and limited use of the research on learning and how people learn as a means of generating different solutions. Part of the problem can also be attributed to the communities the education systems serve, the parents, the corporate sector, and other agencies that have a role to play regarding the welfare and development of children.

How would our communities respond to our doctors if we found that they ignored relevant research in their field, avoided training in the latest methodology, resisted changes to practice, accepted mortality rates of 15 to 30 percent (i.e., failure ratio in school) and directly attributed or assigned blame for these mortality rates to the patient? There would be a great outcry for the doctors to improve their practice. Why should the expectations be any different with education and educators?

Focusing only on achievement and performance of learners will not lead to systemic change. Part of the problem is that many teachers don't have the skill sets and knowledge to teach math and literacy, to teach real-world skills in an applied setting, or to teach critical and analytical thinking to all students. Nor are the correct models for training, leadership, governance, curriculum, and assessment in place to support the new classroom and instructional practices that have yet to be developed. Those new practices will be shaped by some of the following realities:

- Technology and science, especially genome research and life sciences, should be considered as important as math and literacy. They are two of the major influences that are reshaping social, political, and economic aspects of the global society.
- In today's world the ability to read, write, and apply information from technical documents is just as important as literature-based literacy. Technical literacy and literature-based literacy are not the same. The skill sets for each are different, unique, and not transferable. In other words, being literate in one area does not make you literate in another.
- Not only are the skill levels for being literate and numeric higher than those in the past, but they must also be redefined. That definition needs to be expanded to also include technology, knowledge about science, especially life sciences, as well as the ability to interpret visual images in both a print and digital format. Some are even suggesting that financial literacy needs to be included in the definition.

These new skills need to be acquired by adults as well as children. The literacy implications for retraining adults throughout North America around these new definitions are significant. One recent study from Canada indicates that 42 percent of the adult population does not posses the literacy skills needed to participate in the information age.[3]

According to ProLiteracy America, "the National Adult Literacy Survey (1993) found that approximately 44 million Americans have extremely limited reading and quantitative skills."[4] But that study appears to have been done within the context of industrial age definitions of literacy. Under information age expectations the numbers would be more significant. When you add in the assessments of young children who come to school unprepared to learn and the number of students who read below grade level at grade four then you see the extent of the problem across North America. These are significant numbers with far-reaching implications for society, the economy, and training and educational services.

But developing new practices is only part of what needs to be done. There must be some effort to create systems, practices, and environments that support, nurture, and sustain change. This was not part of the change process thinking in the late 1980s and early 1990s, and it was a strategic mistake.

Changing the process includes the creation of the form, function, and practice that sustain learning and knowledge building, integration, and acquisition. Focusing on only one element at a time as a means of reforming the education system, such as curriculum, assessment, or middle schools, will continue to be ineffective. All of these things need to be under review as part of the change process. Nothing should be sacrosanct in this review.

It is time to quit fiddling with the past. The standard-bearers of industrial age organizations need to step aside if they are unwilling or unable to focus on what needs to be done. Their attempts to improve the existing structure over the past two decades have not worked. Their misplaced efforts have left our society with a public education system that is vulnerable, dysfunctional, and increasingly irrelevant to far too many students.

The task for change cannot be left in the hands of the uninformed and unknowing. But as Shakespeare wrote: "Aye, there's the rub."[5] Why? The reason is that the industrial age paradigm is incompatible with the information age paradigm. The very nature of the industrial system forces compliance, albeit sometimes slowly, to its ideal and design. Any implementation that is incremental or piecemeal will fail. The challenge in creating a massive and significant change, transcendence versus transformation, is a huge challenge but there is no other way.

To continue with the existing strategies for change borders on incompetence. People need to be vigilant and on guard against *articulate incompetents* who continue to send a message that they know what they are doing. It is clear from the lack of change and the continued downward spiral of industrial age organizations, including the education system, that they do not. They employ a dissociative model of decision making in which decisions are made in spite of the facts.

North Americans are in competition with people from around the globe who are not trapped by an industrial age past. These people are open to new ideas and thoughts that we have been reluctant to consider. Unless we change, their success will result in our failure.

New models of thinking need to be developed that parallel the embrace of the industrial age by the United States in the late 1700s—with a citizenry desirous to create the practice, form, and function for industrial organizations leading to economic prosperity and a better quality of life. The new thinking for that time, coupled with the political, social, and economic will to move forward, paved the way for growth, innovation, and unparalleled economic, political, and social development. The equivalent societal process for the twenty-first century needs to evolve. Only this time the design, form, function, and practice needs to be tied to the information age, not the industrial age.

NOTES

1. Johann Wolfgang von Goethe, BrainyQuote, www.brainyquote.com/quotes/quotes/j/johannwolf150520.html.
2. Bill Gates, (keynote address, National Education Summit on High Schools, February 26, 2005), www.gatesfoundation.org/MediaCenter/Speeches/Co-ChairSpeeches/BillgSpeeches/BGSpeechNGA-050226.htm?version=print.
3. Canadian Council on Learning, "The State of Learning in Canada: No Time for Complacency," *Report on Learning in Canada 2007* (Ottawa: 2007), 3.
4. "U.S. Adult Literacy Programs: Making a Difference," *U.S. Programs Division of ProLiteracy Worldwide*, March 2003, 1.
5. William Shakespeare, *Hamlet*, act 3, scene 1, Folger Shakespeare Library, www.folger.edu/template.cfm?cid=474.

Chapter Two

The Fat Lady Has Sung

If we open a quarrel between the past and the present, we shall find we have lost the future.[1]

The philosophical roots of the industrial age are found in the thinking of René Descartes and Adam Smith. Organizations and systems evolved and grew from the belief that the pieces were more important than the whole and that organizations and systems were a loosely knit aggregation of these parts.

René Descartes, the seventeenth-century philosopher, called upon people to "doubt what isn't self-evident, and reduce every problem to its simplest components."[2] Adam Smith wrote the *Wealth of Nations* in 1776. He said that efficiencies were gained and production increased when industrial work is "broken down into the simplest and basic tasks."[3]

Manufacturers and entrepreneurs who organized their business around this type of thinking helped the United States move ahead of Britain as a world power in the early 1800s. The new economics and thinking resulted in unprecedented industrial growth and the emergence of a Western culture, built around affluence, material wealth, and innovation.

Natural resources provided the fuel to manufacture as well as the raw material to create products. The development of specialties, bodies of knowledge, skills, and processes influenced the organizational function, practices, and procedures. This created a culture and a system that was unique to the industrial age era.

The emphasis on industrialization and on innovations and changes brought great success to many in the United States for most of the nineteenth and twentieth centuries. Now these systems and organizations struggle to be competitive in today's environment of rapid and different change. The rules for the continued survival of these systems and organizations are different from

15

the ones that assisted in their formation. Much of what worked in the nineteenth and twentieth centuries is not sustainable in the twenty-first century.

To be successful and change implies a willingness to accept the challenge to learn and understand new things. It also implies a willingness to unlearn that which is no longer useful or valid. Changing the way we work, learn, organize, and use information will be the fundamental outcome of this process. It is not enough to try to fix old practices within the industrial age paradigm. Being more productive and efficient at past practice is of little value in an information age environment.

Our public education systems were shaped by the industrial age world of work or, as some individuals would say, the *real world*. The curriculum development, instructional pedagogy, classroom practice, and the structure and organization owe their form and substance to industrial age thinking. The public school employs an assembly line approach to production. The curriculum for subjects like math and English are organized into specialized areas of study over thirteen years or grades. Learning takes place in modules dictated by time, not mastery.

Those who master what needs to be learned are called graduates. The assumption is that the *pieces* or the grades, after thirteen years of instruction, will provide learners with a set of coordinated learning experiences that in turn create the educated citizen for industrial age times.

In contrast, the organizing idea for the information age is completely different. This new thinking recognizes the importance of pieces (analysis) and specialized bodies of knowledge but requires that information be aggregated and synthesized in a systemic way in order to create, build, develop, integrate, and apply knowledge among, between, and within systems. These are the major functions of knowledge-based organizations.

Information is the key resource of this age. Knowledge, meaning, and application are the products. New organizational function, practices, and procedures are required to support, nurture, and create the organizational structure and culture needed to sustain knowledge-based organizations. If Descartes and Smith provided the philosophical *raison d'être* for the industrial age, then Marshall McLuhan, *Understanding Media: The Extensions of Man,*[4] and Alvin Toffler, *The Third Wave,*[5] might be their information age counterparts.

In the industrial age organization, personal and group power is sustained by not sharing information outside the area of your specialization. In the information age, personal and organization power are enhanced when information and knowledge are shared across the system. The research on learning, and how people learn, is the building block for creating and applying knowledge. This research is also critical to the discussion about creating learning systems. Learning systems might replace educational systems. It means developing a new context for curriculum design, instructional pedagogy, classroom practice, the shape and function of organizations, leadership, governance, communication, decision making, the use of technology, and partnerships. These are the insights that demonstrate how different the information age is from the industrial age. Learning, and how people learn, becomes the lens for viewing and creating the design, shape, and function of all aspects of the organization in a knowledge-based society and economy. If information is the driver of the knowledge-based society and its economy, then learning is its engine.

But the learning systems or organizations we need to properly support the trends and realities of this new paradigm are still in the embryo stage. Pieces are in place but more needs to be done. Trying to shift to something new within the present environment is chaotic. The past, present, and future are colliding.

Representative groups within the system are consumed by a debate on *what is* and *what was* instead of focusing on *what should be*. The collision of ideas, thoughts, and beliefs is resulting in confusion, chaos, dysfunction, and inactivity within education systems and indeed within society. This only serves to block the development of any meaningful change initiative that can move us from the past into the future in a meaningful and systemic manner.

The boomer generation was raised to believe that a healthy, vibrant, relevant public education system was the cornerstone of democratic life. Attention to studies, good marks on exams, and an industrious attitude would unlock doors to whatever you wanted to achieve in life. In retrospect, one can certainly see what was right and wrong with that approach. For all of its faults, that system was instrumental in sustaining and maintaining a high quality of life for most of us over the past number of decades. But now the rules are changing and we must be prepared to change with them.

There can be no consensus as to how to reform the education system when there is no common understanding as to what has changed and why. Our society is witness to some very tumultuous times due to technology: the emergence of new economies, global trends, and political upheavals and unrest. The status quo is changing. Some people see this change as evidence that our society is in a downward spiral. Many people are becoming aware that the beliefs, skills, and understandings they use to work and live are no longer adequate. Many people in the middle class are finding that past practice, learning, and experience are not transferable to the new economy. This has great implications for the society, especially for those who are unemployed or just out of school and looking for work.

This begs the question for which there is no clear answer as yet. If a competent public education system is the means by which people gain access to and opportunity for a quality lifestyle, why is there no urgency to reform public education? If the education system is preparing people for a past that is no longer relevant, why would we not change it?

Is it that we don't care or that we are too involved in our own personal work to worry about the needs of others? Have we reached a time in our culture where we think that only the *best* should be educated? Perhaps if more people understood the implications of a failed education system to their individual and collective social, political, and economic well-being, they would not be so complacent about the current state of affairs. The following examples demonstrate how the system is failing to serve the needs of all students:

- There is a trend in various jurisdictions both in Canada and the United States to limit access to postsecondary institutions. In the name of standards these policymakers are introducing tougher graduation requirements and in some cases, higher tuition costs. But that which they represent as reform and higher standards is really *smoke and mirrors*. They are only shifting the goal posts. What they are really doing is screening and making sure that only the top 15 percent or so of students are eligible to gain access to their institutions.
- These entry requirements are less about standards and more about economics. There are not enough seats at postsecondary institutions for all who qualify and some of those who do qualify can't afford to attend. On one hand access is being limited and on the other there is no counter initiative to provide alternative and meaningful educational experiences for those not going into the postsecondary system. It is as if we are prepared to limit the opportunity and potential contributions of a whole generation of young people, both in secondary and postsecondary institutions.
- There are a number of exemplary technology trades and school-to-work programs, for example, in secondary schools around North America. Students in these programs are not bound for university but are being well served in terms of their future. They are being provided with a set of skills that will make them employable and allow them access to quality lifestyles. But these programs are not systemic or universal across public education systems. As a consequence, student access to these programs and services is happenstance. This, at a time when corporations are approaching government complaining that they need to import skilled workers from other countries because the existing system is not providing them. This is a travesty.

That far too many students are ending up without the skills to function, work, and learn in our society should be a cause for alarm. A generation of unemployable and low-skilled individuals places a significant drag on the economy and the society. With the right programs and incentives, the need for skilled trade and technology workers could be met within existing structures. One is left to ponder the reasons for such an oversight. Could it be some social engineers have shown that it is cheaper to recruit workers from other countries then to train them within our own education systems?

Thomas L. Friedman wrote an article for the *New York Times*, based on his book *The World Is Flat: A Brief History of the Twenty-First Century,* in which he describes how global technology systems have shrunk or flattened the world, creating global access and competition to things that used to be the purview of the Western world, particularly the United States.[6] He makes the point that "we are developing an education gap. Here is the dirty little secret that no C.E.O. wants to tell you: they are not just outsourcing to save on salary. They are doing it because they can often get better-skilled and more productive people than their American workers."

Does the concept of the global economy and wealth override national governments and does the business agenda drive political, educational, and economic agendas to the point that our democratic values and way of life are at stake? If skills and attitudes need to be adjusted, certainly that should be possible. That is not an appropriate rationale for not educating our young. Perhaps a better rationale can be found in Thomas Jefferson's caution about merchants. It is worthy of some reflection. He said, "Merchants have no country. The mere spot they stand in does not constitute so strong an attachment as that from which they draw their gains."[7]

Certainly change is needed in the attitude that some students have toward work and the importance of learning. For these students there is a sense of apathy toward learning. They see no connection between what happens in school and what will happen in their lives. The answer might rest in Bill Gates's observation that the secondary school is obsolete. Perhaps a large percentage of the young recognize that the industrial age school is not relevant to what they need. They can see what is wrong but haven't quite reached the point to see what needs to change.

By any measure this is an unhealthy trend and will have serious and long-term consequences. When a business loses clients it does everything it can to regain lost customers. If it doesn't, it usually goes under. We need that same sense of urgency within public education so that we start doing what needs to be done.

The system also fails students when it uses its resources and expertise to keep the system focused on reforms that will have little impact. The reform must be structured within a context that aims at changing the core business of the educational enterprise. This is seldom the case. The following are examples of reforms or processes that continue to enshrine the past and inhibit renewal:

- Technology is often profiled in change initiatives. It is as if the addition of technology to any initiative automatically qualifies it as being futuristic. Yet in most cases the technology is being used to enhance past practice. Technology itself can't create the changes we need in education. The focus for change has to be on the education system itself and the underlying notions that sustain it. Technology has yet to be used in a way that creates new practice, form, and function in the classroom or school.
- The present model for the implementation of social programs is a source of concern. Educational dollars intended for the delivery of educational programs have been diverted toward social reforms including such things as hot lunch programs, school safety, drug awareness, child abuse, access to information legislation, bullying, and harassment. These programs are seldom funded by new money. The centralized bureaucracies usually make cuts to programs and services for learners to fund these initiatives. The question is not about the validity of these programs but about the validity of using scarce educational dollars to bring about social, rather than educational, change at a time when educational change is paramount to the future of the society.
- Bullying, drug abuse, and harassment can't be fixed at school without addressing the same issues in the home and the community. Communities need to look inward at their own social behaviors and attitudes and take responsibility for them. Neither the problem, nor the solution, rests with the school, but with the community as a whole. The school is merely a mirror of what is happening in the community. Drug use, abuse, and harassment don't just happen at school.

Public education systems have an incurable disease—incurable as long as the guardians of the medicine cabinet are politicians and self-serving power groups within the traditional hierarchy of the educational delivery systems.

Not only do we continue to prepare learners for the past but we also measure their success according to benchmarks that are no longer relevant. The data merchants who work for the centralized bureaucracies continue to quantify and measure how well we are doing at past practice and shape the results to fit political agendas. They do this because the information they provide is what the public understands and knows because of their own school experience.

A relevant and competent public education system is based on "a democracy of opportunity and an aristocracy of achievement."[8] If people still believe that a public education system is the cornerstone of our democracy as well as the doorway to societal access and opportunity, then we have a lot of work to do.

Creating and sustaining a new public education system that is aligned with the new age is a significant task. It means that all of society must be involved and the reform of the system can't be left to those within the system who have the most to win or lose by change. If reform is left in the hands of special interest groups then the needs of learners will never come first. The primary concern of these special interests is to protect and support those delivering the service and ensure that no serious consequence befalls anyone unless they are involved in criminal activity. Change, relevance, and performance in the classroom have not been an organizational priority, but that no longer is a sustainable option.

This means that any reform process is as much the responsibility of those who deliver, govern, and finance the services, as it is those who receive those services or benefit from them. This requires the creation of community-based processes designed to support, encourage, and resource the reform because the reform of public education also speaks to the reform of community. One cannot happen without the other.

There is a popular sports expression that says, "It ain't over 'til the fat lady sings."[9] For public education and the society it serves, *the fat lady has sung*. There is very little time left to do what we need to do. Change will happen with or without our participation. If we wish to sustain a way of life that embraces and promotes a positive and hopeful future, then we as a people need to focus on the substantial reform of public education.

NOTES

1. Winston Churchill, www.anglik.net/churchill.htm.

2. Quoted in James Burke, "Inventors and Inventions, Accidents plus Luck: The Sum of Innovation Is Greater Than Its Parts." *Time Magazine*, December 4, 2000.

3. Quoted in Michael Hammer and James Champy, *Reengineering the Corporation* (New York: HarperCollins, 1994), p. 2.

4. Marshall McLuhan, *Understanding Media: The Extensions of Man* (New York: McGraw-Hill, 1964).

5. Alvin Toffler, *The Third Wave* (New York: Morrow, 1980).

6. Thomas L. Friedman, "It's a Flat World After All," *New York Times,* April 3, 2005.

7. Thomas Jefferson, BrainyQuote, www.brainyquote.com/quotes/quotes/t/q138493.html.

8. Anon (falsely attributed to Thomas Jefferson), Jefferson Library at Monticello, www.monticello.org/library/reference/spurious.html.

9. Dan Cook, during a sports newscast in April 1978, quoted in "Dear Abby," *San Francisco Chronicle,* November 22, 1987, www.santacruzpl.org/readyref/files/d-f/fat.shtml.

Chapter Three

That Was Then—This Might Be Now

I am not interested in preserving the status quo; I want to overthrow it.[1]

The following scenario is a somewhat futuristic, albeit plausible, view of family life in the twenty-first century. This scenario describes a mismatch between the skills required to survive and thrive in the world of work and those provided to the family's daughter, Susan, enrolled in a public elementary school.

Jason awoke to the gentle sounds of waves lapping at a pebble beach. It was one of the environmental features of the *smart* home that he and his family had moved into; a home that had the latest in converging technologies that supported the family's work, learning, and lifestyle. Jason had selected the background sound from one of the programming consoles located around the home. He used it as a means of helping him transition peacefully from sleep to full consciousness. Once awake, he activated a program on his personal digital assistant that gave him an auditory summary of his tasks for the day, including conferences and appointments.

Jason was known for his skills and abilities as a knowledge engineer. He worked with teams of specialists around the world (sometimes online, through two-way interactive conferences, and face-to-face meetings) to develop new projects or concepts especially pertaining to genetic research. Although not a content specialist in any given area, Jason was skilled in the processes of facilitating ideas and innovations, identifying key concepts that transformed an idea into reality, decision making, product development, and project assessment. He also designed the training and processes needed to integrate the new knowledge across the system as well as what knowledge needed to be deleted or unlearned. His wife, who was up three hours earlier to facilitate an online conference on water quality from their home communication studio, was an environmental specialist.

Normally, Jason would begin his day with an exercise program and work with an online fitness expert who would guide him through his routines, provide feedback, and suggest adjustments to his dietary program. Part of the process included weekly assessment of heart rate, blood pressure, and home analysis of urine and blood samples to determine sugar levels and cholesterol counts. This data was programmed into a home database that both he and his online mentor could review and use as a reference point for dietary and exercise decisions.

Jean, his wife, had sent a message to his personal digital assistant asking Jason to join the family on the patio for breakfast. To accommodate this, he rescheduled his exercise program for later in the day.

While in the shower he activated the *smart screen* embedded in the shower wall and received information from the personalized information system to which he subscribed. He quickly scanned his stock portfolio, noted key developments in various stock markets around the globe, and received information on new innovations in the field of genetics and technology, as well as summaries of key news stories in the areas of politics, the arts, and human interest he had selected. Unable to review all of the information while showering, he transferred it to the wall screen in his bedroom and watched and listened to the rest of the program while he dressed.

Upon entering the patio, he greeted his wife and family who were already seated. The food was on the table and the *smart tablecloth* kept the juice cold and the waffles warm. During breakfast, the family engaged in a number of environmental and values discussions around issues related to Jean's interactive conference. Debate and discussion were always encouraged as part of the family interaction along with a caveat for manners, fair play, respect, and rational arguments.

On a whim, Jason asked if the family would like to go to a movie. Tonight was the premier showing of the latest Hollywood blockbuster that was being transmitted digitally throughout North America to local cinemas. Their son, Jim, quickly went online, confirmed that they could get four tickets, selected their preferred seats, and enacted the purchase. Within seconds, the confirmation and tickets were being printed.

Before finishing breakfast, Jean reviewed the family messaging protocol. She reminded everyone to use their cell phones or computers to post messages to the *information board* if they were going to be delayed or needed to do something else that was not known at this time. It was a family expectation that each member of the household would post their schedule for others to see and keep everyone informed of changes to that schedule.

After the kids left for school, Jason and Jean had another cup of coffee. It was an opportunity to access the garden design software they had been using over the past few months to create a cactus garden off the patio. They were satisfied with the design and forwarded it to three horticulturist firms they had researched, asking for quotes. Jean also took the opportunity to call up the website for a boutique she frequented. Her personalized mannequin appeared, resulting from a thirty-second scan of her body during her last visit to the store. She had selected a blouse, skirt, and scarf, which now appeared on the mannequin. Jason and Jean discussed fit, color, and style as Jean tried various outfits and combinations. Finally satisfied, she placed an order and received a confirmation that the selections would be created that day and delivered by courier to her door by 3:30 that afternoon.

Jean also reminded Jason to meet her at the Fairfax Elementary School for a scheduled parent–teacher meeting that afternoon regarding their daughter, Susan.

Jason went to his office and, after a brief videoconference with his financial advisor and making some small adjustments to his portfolios, accessed his voice mails, emails, and faxes. After responding to his messages and adjusting his schedule, he began a series of conferences with his online teams.

He completed some quotations for potential clients who had accessed his website, researched the online law library for some advice on a contractual issue, and responded to two potential advertisers who wanted to support his website. After searching some sites and comparing costs, he purchased two tickets for him and Jean to attend a conference in San Antonio, booked a hotel, and made reservations for dinner following his keynote presentation. He also arranged for a car rental so that he and Jean could take two weeks of vacation in the Texas Gulf.

Before leaving for the parent–teacher meeting, he went to the console in the kitchen, adjusted the lighting for various rooms, identified two television programs he wished to record, checked the security features for the house, programmed the robotic lawn mower and vacuum cleaner, set the watering schedule for the lawn, and put on some light mood music.

He had never been to Fairfax Elementary School. The move to their new home had precipitated a change in schools for Susan. He checked the map, entered the address of the school in the global positioning unit in the car, hit the self-adjusting environmental control, and selected a series of favorite songs from his iPod.

His wife was already at the school when he arrived. There were few children around at this time of day. He noted that the school was reminiscent in design, shape, and color of the elementary school he attended some twenty-five years ago.

He saw the sign that indicated that he should report to the office. He did so and was directed to his daughter's classroom. He noted the computer on the secretary's desk, the PA system behind the secretary, and the filing cabinets for storage of records.

As he moved down the hallways, he looked at the black and white boards, filled with written information, on the walls of the classroom. He also noted the display boards of children's artwork and neatly written and printed displays of poetry. As he passed by classrooms, he saw various configurations of furniture to accommodate individual and group work.

Upon entering the class he found his wife and the teacher, Ms. Gregory, engaged in conversation. As he moved to the teacher's desk at the front of the room, he also noted collections of textbooks and resources along the wall, as well as four computers located at the back of the room.

The conversation regarding Susan was thorough, professional, and friendly. Susan was doing well in school and the teacher was obviously knowledgeable about Susan's performance and about her as a person.

Susan read well, was numeric, and wrote well, although her spelling was judged as only fair. She had a good grasp of social studies curriculum but didn't seem to like science. Her assignments were always handed in on time. The teacher found her to be friendly, mannerly, and socially well adjusted. Questions about her acquisition of technological skills received a response from the teacher of not enough equipment, support, or training in the school, as well as concerns about a lack of infrastructure and poor connectivity. Information was also presented regarding the school's initiatives regarding safety, drug awareness, hot lunch programs, equity, dealing with bullying, and reading.

As Jason left the school and began his journey home, he recognized that he was concerned by what he had just experienced but was not sure why. Surely Susan was, by all accounts, a well-adjusted individual who was doing well in most things and could do better in some others. What then was the problem?

He started to reflect on his day and the environment in which he and his wife worked in. He reflected on the skills, attitudes, and attributes they both needed to be successful in this environment. He then compared that to the profile he was just given of Susan and started to recognize the mismatch. It became clear to him that Susan was doing well but some of her skill acquisition, and more important, the skills she was not acquiring, would leave her prepared for a time that had already passed. The time she was being prepared for was still represented in the school but not in their home or lifestyle.

The issues were more than access and use of technology, although the school appeared to be substantially behind in technological services, programs, and options that were readily available at home. Jason's concern was about the skill sets needed to utilize the convergence of technologies in the home along with the integration of process and content skills to acquire, build upon, and/or create knowledge that were missing. The home was about learning to learn, about adapting to rapid change, and about using information/knowledge to create, build, share, and apply. The school was about mastering a specific set of curriculum outcomes; outcomes that were very similar to what Jason learned in elementary school.

The parent–teacher meeting spoke to Susan's proficiency in a number of subject areas including literacy and numeracy. It also spoke to her work habits and attitudes but what it didn't report on was perhaps more important. There was no mention of such things as:

* the acquisition/application of technological skills for learning;
* the acquisition of a mindset to work;
* awareness of the importance of genetic and environmental science;
* exposure to what it might mean to live and learn in the new environments of the *fiber state*;
* acquiring deeper levels of knowledge and application beyond the mastery level;
* the ability to make ethical decisions in a topsy-turvy environment;
* the ability to work face-to-face and online with teams;
* the ability to be independent, creative, and a critical thinker;
* the development of an attitude about being effective and thoughtful citizens in this new age;
* knowledge of learning and learning processes; nor
* technical, digital, and financial literacy.

Susan was receiving some instruction on process and technological skills, but it was delivered in an isolated and fragmentary way. She was learning about and preparing for the future at home, and educated for the past at school.

If Susan's education was not providing the skills, attitudes, and attributes needed to work and learn in the new paradigm, what then were her future chances for success? Jason felt that he and his wife had done a good job of preparing Susan for school but that the skill set and attitudes needed to work and live in their home had little connection with what the school was doing.

For Jason, it was a paradox. In school, his daughter was well cared for. School staff ensured that she was safe and protected. She was encouraged and supported in her learning by her teachers and she was attaining appropriate, or better, levels of proficiency in what she learned.

As he entered the driveway, it finally became clear. Their home was the reality of the twenty-first century whereas the reality of the school was that of the previous century. The school was delivering an education around the mastery of content in specified areas and the dispensing of information. The home on the other hand was using a variety of information sources to nurture learning and create, build, share, and interpret knowledge, as well as to create meaning and application from that knowledge. The practice, thinking, organization, and mindset needed to function in the home were nowhere to be found in the school. The school was a museum that paid homage to the practice, form, and function of its industrial past.

NOTE

1. Niccolo Machiavelli, ThinkExist.com, thinkexist.com/quotation/i-m_not_interested_in_preserving_the_status_quo-i/148838.html.

Chapter Four

Five Perspectives on Education

Sweet are the uses of adversity.[1]

When any group, be it a sports team, an organization, a political party, or a corporation, achieves outstanding success, its members seldom force themselves to reflect, rethink, and change that which brought them the success. They tend to enshrine and sustain that which has made them successful. The people who delivered ice, for example, did not understand the impact refrigeration would have on their livelihood. The owners of railways did not understand the significance of air travel. And the people on the deck of the *Titanic* could not comprehend that their lives were at risk and that the ship was sinking. They didn't think that it was possible.

In all of these cases, individual or collective beliefs kept people *frozen in time* so to speak. They understood the nature of what they were doing but never recognized any internal or external threats or challenges that would affect their continued safety or well-being. They were unwilling or unable to adapt or adopt new behaviors, practice, or thinking. They were surprised by new and unanticipated realities because they relied on their past to interpret their future.

Responding to threats or change seems to have more to do initially with emotion or feeling than it has to do with logic. In this environment, any change that is seen to have clear benefit or improvement for the individual or group is likely to be embraced. If the proposed change threatens beliefs, practice, or position in the social or organizational structure, it is likely to be resisted.

The assumptions, perceptions, and beliefs that inform emotion or feelings are the greatest barriers or obstacles to implementing any significant change. Consequently, before one can begin a discussion about what educational systems are or should be, one must first consider and evaluate some of the beliefs that drive the system.

There are at least five, sometimes competing, perspectives that influence our present public education systems. The first four are driven by industrial age beliefs and clearly favor sustaining the status quo. The fifth is driven by information age beliefs and calls for something quite different from what we have at present. They are as follows:

1. Education was of more value to citizens and reflected a higher standard of achievement in the previous decades than it does today. People who hold this perspective desire no major change to the structure, delivery, management, and governance of education. Their concern is to get public education *back on track*, by emphasizing basics, establishing consistent and appropriate standards for achievement, and assessing system performance to meet so-called accountability expectations.
2. Public education is the medium for the reconstruction of a society that is not functioning as well as it should. The people who hold this perspective are generally not educators. They are social engineers who demand that educational resources, both human and financial, be allocated to remedying society's ills through school-based programs.

   These programs are designed to deal with issues like bullying, hunger, harassment, safety, diversity, social justice, and racism. There is an assumption that the basics of education will be delivered no matter what, and that any reform of the system should address social not instructional/achievement issues.
3. The third perspective pertains to power and control of the system. It resides in the thinking, practice, and leadership of the various stakeholders within public education. These groups, be they parents, boards, district staff, school-based administration, unions, or organizations of special interest like librarians, technologists, or special services, see their roles as distinct and separate from each other.

   For each group, the role or function of the other groups is viewed as an impediment or in competition for that which they wish to accomplish. This creates a dynamic whereby each group is trying to gain the balance of power within the system. When defending their positions or voicing their opinion, the rhetoric of these groups is often cloaked in the language of what is best for children. In reality children are not the priority and each group is really advocating for itself.
4. An increasing percentage of the public views public education as being too hopelessly mired in political wrangling to be effective. People who feel this way seek alternatives to public education and see the expansion of the school choice agenda as the only way they can assure their children access to a productive future and a sustainable way of life. The people who hold

this perspective are often industrial in their thinking. They recognize that public education is in trouble but look to the past for solutions—a past free from politics, with defined values, and embracing industrial definitions of rigor.

5. The fifth and final perspective is the least common of the five. It holds that public education systems have served us well, but as the industrial age era ends and a new paradigm emerges, something different is needed. People who hold this perspective do not believe that a system steeped in industrial practice, form, and function can be reformed or adapted to meet the needs of a twenty-first-century society dependent on knowledge and learning. They believe that the system structure must be re-created or transcended.

This book is obviously biased toward the fifth perspective but creating change around that reality is proving to be quite difficult. The task of creating meaningful change is significant. The human experience suggests that many people will continue to find ways to avoid or ignore the consequences of this type of change. Recent studies showed that two-thirds of Americans were unprepared for a major disaster[2] and that many were unprepared for another terrorist attack.[3] It took twenty years of constant messaging before a majority of people in the USA started using seatbelts despite the overwhelming evidence to the contrary.[4] Having facts and knowledge about something does not always lead to informed decision making or a change in practice and/or behavior.

People who use catchphrases like "If it ain't broke, don't fix it" suspend their thought processes about reforming public education by doing so and avoid having to consider the implications of maintaining the status quo. But these *keepers of the quo* should be disabused of their notions and come to grips with the implications of their views to our collective future if they fail to engage in the challenge of change.

NOTES

1. William Shakespeare, *As You Like It*, act 2, scene 1, 12–17, enotes.com, www.enotes.com/shakespeare-quotes/sweet-uses-adversity.
2. http://www.usatoday.com/news/nation/2007-05-09-emergencies_N.htm.
3. http://www.acep.org/pressroom.aspx?id=25590.
4. http://www.harrisinteractive.com/news/allnewbydate/aspNewsID=568.

Chapter Five

We Are What We Were

The best thing about the future is that it comes only one day at a time.[1]

To some people the need for widespread change to our education systems is very clear. But having an agreement on the need for change does not mean there is agreement on what to change. There are no common agreed upon reference points within our society to guide our actions and thinking about the learning system we need. If we did agree to the content or substance of change we would find that there is little understanding as to the processes we need to follow to arrive at those outcomes. Given that the basic unit of change in a knowledge-based society is the individual mind, perhaps the starting point for enacting change is to ensure that all citizens are provided with the opportunity to acquire the needed skills, knowledge, and insights to participate. But that type of an engagement is a challenge.

It seems that the less we know about something that interests us the more likely we are to gather more knowledge and understanding about the topic. Because it is *new learning*, we are generally more open to information and knowledge that may challenge our existing beliefs and the more likely we are to change our thinking. Conversely, the more we understand and know something, especially if it has contributed to our personal or organizational success, the more likely we are to resist any challenges to what we believe and practice. We are likely to be closed to anything that challenges our beliefs or requires us to think differently.

Adults who have spent thirteen years in the public education system are inculcated to its values and beliefs, thereby ensuring a consistency in expectations, support, and understanding for the current public education system. In many cases, this experience has influenced their success as workers and citizens. It is what they know and they will be reluctant to consider and re-flect upon new ideas.

This mindset has prevented any meaningful systemic discussion or dia-logue about reform or changes within the education system or within the communities it serves. When people are knowledgeable and comfortable with their past and successful because of it, it is hard to convince them to consider changing what they have come to know and believe.

The public education system has been feeling pressure to change for at least two decades. For the most part the system has been able to control and restrict the agenda of change. But events and circumstances are beginning to shift the focus of the control away from the system and into the *unknown*. The system is more and more on the defensive. Politicians, bureaucrats, and ad-ministrators at many levels are assuring their publics that they are responding to the issues and that all is well, or will be. But all is not well.

Students are graduating from secondary schools with many of the same cur-riculum experiences their parents had, with the possible exception of senior math and science. One has only to reflect on the rapid and dramatic changes taking place in almost every aspect of our society and ask, how can that be? How can our public education systems remain immune and distant from the substantive changes needed to help individuals be conversant with and successful in a twenty-first-century society and economy? And, how can we continue to point to past practice and say that is what our children and our communities need?

Over the past decade globalization has resulted in the loss of community services, a reduction in lifestyle, particularly for the middle class, and a loss of jobs in many parts of North America. Yet despite all of this, education, and the society it serves, continues to turn to its past as a means of responding to the issues. It is as if we believe that if we restore educational services to the perceived standards that served generations gone by, we will have *saved the day*. This type of thinking does not make sense.

The reality we face is substantial and threatening. We have arrived at a mo-ment in time that signals the need for new organizations and systems.

Many organizations have tried to restructure themselves over the past two decades, some with more success than others. The *writing had been on the wall* for quite a period of time, yet these organizations and systems failed to respond until they were in crises. The culminating events that caused the fall of the Berlin Wall, and put IBM, GM, Ford, and Chrysler on the brink of financial dis-aster are rooted in the same realities and conditions that currently affect public education systems. The same may be said of the mortgage crises, the fall of Lehman Brothers, and the reorganization of Merrill Lynch and AIG.

The industrial age culture, by its very nature, seeks to control the change process. Change in this environment is slow and incremental. The organizational focus is on the product, on the specialized knowledge, and on the organizational piece. Organizational excellence or failure is defined by the financial bottom line. It is a narrow perspective. There is seldom a focus on the organization as a whole, on its current state of relevancy and competency, on how the pieces interact, or on the leveraging of organizational knowledge in a systemic way. Government agencies, departments, or ministries are structured around this type of thinking and are major contributors to the reason our society is unable to quickly adapt or change. The information age culture is different. It promotes a systemic view, honors learning, values knowledge, is fast moving and evolving, and defines the relationship between both product and process, as well as the pieces and the whole. This culture promotes consideration of partnerships between and among systems that are of mutual benefit.

Organizations in this new environment have to be flexible, adaptable, and able to evolve quickly. Appropriate risk taking by individuals and groups is encouraged as is knowledge building and knowledge sharing across the system. Excellence in these organizations is defined in terms of both product and process. They need to be systemically integrated to create, change, improve, or develop an outcome.

History, for the most part, is a chronicle of events and outcomes that reflect upon humankind's ability or inability to adjust to new realities. Our past is full of examples of historic events that have oftentimes resulted in consequences of tragic proportion because of our inability to change, adapt, or accommodate. This may be the Achilles' heel of North American society. This inability to change, adapt, or accommodate is apparent in the following observation.

John Milton was sympathetic to Galileo's discoveries but was caught in a contradiction between his religious beliefs and Galileo's discoveries. Milton wrote *Paradise Lost* around his religious beliefs. He was "unable or unwilling to revise his thought to match the newly discovered universe" defined by Galileo.[2] Within public education systems, we know a lot about learning and how people learn but we seem to be unable or unwilling to revise our education system and our instructional practices to match what we know. Practice does not reflect research.

In the industrial age organization the tasks, functions, and structures are there to serve the needs of those in the organization. They were initially intended to support and nourish the core purpose for that organization's existence. This becomes a point of conflict in the organization, when an idea or innovation is introduced that serves the core purpose of the organization but threatens existing practices or procedures that serve the well-being of those who deliver the service.

Public education systems were influenced by the ideas of René Descartes, Adam Smith, Thomas Jefferson, Henry Ford, and Alfred Sloan. Their influence is seen in the organization of work, the development of governance and policy, leadership programs, and management systems, as well as the process of strategic planning, accountability processes, and evaluation. Their influence is also seen in the notion of grades, in school organization and timetables, in management structures, and in the organization of curriculum and learning outcomes. But after two hundred years of development, the continued existence of the system is being threatened by forces both internal and external to the system. The following is a consideration of the nature and form of four of those threats:

1. The first threat is found in attitudes. Over the past decade we have seen the emergence of a public that knows what they want and when they want it in terms of personal products and services. They are not necessarily satisfied or content with receiving only what organizations and institutions are prepared to give them. As members of the *I/me* generation, they are more concerned with their own needs than those of the people around them.

   They like choice. As the demands for customized service increase, industrial age systems, including public education, have shown that they are not able to adapt or accommodate requests for products or services that vary from the norm. This does not mean that the public is particularly well informed about what is changing, and why, within the society. They are not acting as advocates for information age learning systems. Instead their view is more egocentric and self-serving. The needs under consideration are personal and not systemic.

2. The second threat to the continued existence of the public education system comes from Internet service providers. They offer customized educational services around what individuals want, when they need it, and in the manner best suited to their personal educational needs.

   The emergence of these online systems if they get it right could be a defining moment for public education. What they presently offer and how they offer it does not represent a new model of education. Instead, they have customized the present system to meet individual need. They are not providing what the society needs in terms of learning, but their existence and success will have an impact, especially at the secondary level. Students who have a need for employment, the need to learn at different times than permitted by the timetable, and who have the self-discipline and the learning skills to work and learn in this environment will opt to do so. So will those who are opposed to the culture of school or who have reasons to be concerned for their personal safety.

   What they are trying to do may well become the impetus for change and reform but at this point in time these web-based offerings should not be confused with educational reform. Many of these new systems utilize information and communication technologies to create an impression of a new educational model. But these models do not generally deal with how people learn. Nor are they designed around the organizing idea for the information age paradigm complete with the skills, attitudes, and beliefs needed to be successful in the world of work, as a learner, or as a citizen. They remain content and not process driven. But they appeal to some people who want choice. Businesses that want access to the vast amount of dollars spent on providing existing educational services see this as an opportunity to compete with public schools for these funds.

3. The third threat comes from a belief by those in the education system that they have a monopoly on providing programs and services. They seem to ignore the growth of private schools, charter schools, and web-based schools. The question about competition for educational dollars would never arise if schools incorporated what is known about learning into their practices and procedures. By doing so they would provide quality learning opportunities for all students. Schools used to be the primary source for dispensing information to the society but the advent of information communication technologies has changed that. Providing information is no longer the schools' area of specialization.

The new area of specialization involves the primacy of learning and its role in acquiring, shaping, applying, and utilizing knowledge. It is the new market niche for education. The potential for developing this niche resides with those in the existing system but it is a time-limited offer. It exists because quality learning is personal, interactive, and best delivered under the leadership of a learning specialist and within a human context, whether face-to-face or in an electronic format. Teachers with new practice and new understandings, supported by organizations and governance structures designed to support learning, are in the best position to develop this new area of specialization. But will they? It remains to be seen if they reinvent themselves, and by doing so, help lead the reinvention of the system.

Educators, in general, rebel at this notion of niche markets and clients. It is an elitist view. They continue to see those who utilize public education services as one group with a common fixed need. This is a strategic error. They need to understand that their monopolistic view of education keeps them from being competitive. And to be competitive they must be prepared to demonstrate a higher standard of performance and service. By doing so, they will help sustain the values and principles behind a quality public education system.

4. The fourth threat to the continuation of the public education system comes from existing divisions within the society. There are inequities in citizenship

when access to educational programs and services are dependent on location and wealth. It is important to the whole society to have an educational system driven by abilities, skills, and learning. Inequitable access to education leads to inequitable access to work and to participation in the society. It becomes a question of affluence and influence instead of expertise and ability. A multitiered education system is not a healthy inducement for sustaining a democracy.

The de facto deregulation of public education allows for a host of alternative offerings. It may be the most pressing social/political issue of the new millennium because of its potential to widen the gap between the haves and have nots. Proposals around voucher systems, the creation of charter schools, the expansion of private schools, the creation of tax credits for attendance at private schools, and a host of alternate delivery services offered in a digital format on the World Wide Web are examples of this deregulation. Perhaps it is the only way to bring the question about the future of education to a crisis. But getting to that point poses huge risks.

The question is not about whether public education systems can change. It should be about what happens if they don't. The *threats* to education are precipitating changes but are they the changes we need? More than learning is at stake. The new public learning organization needs to be based upon the concepts of learning and the learning community. Content, processes, and the technology of the organization must become areas of equal value within the community of learners. This requires a look at the new nature of work and how it impacts on the core business of the organization because the knowledge economy of the 21st century is clearly aligned with new models of work and learning.

The nature of work in schools has remained constant over many decades as it has in most other industrial jobs. For the past twenty years the business community has touted the so-called business revolution to show how they have accommodated to changing times. In most cases, they have used information age tools only to enhance industrial age practice.

Frederick Taylor, for example, created processes around scientific principles at the turn of the twentieth century as a means of increasing a worker's productivity.[3] He was applying scientific thinking to industrial age concepts of work. His assumption was that the worker needed to be closely supervised as a means of improving productivity. This concept is very much part of the culture of school.

This perceived need for close supervision has led some organizations to use information and communication technologies to monitor desktop productivity and time at task in ways that were never possible before. Taylor's principles about improving industrial work concepts are implemented to a greater degree than ever before. An information age tool has been used to strengthen an industrial age concept.

These information/communication technologies have been adapted by business, but they are not being used to create the form, function, and practice needed in the information age paradigm. To some degree the centralized systems that control education are employing assessment and accountability measures to accomplish that same goal. Alfred Sloan, with General Motors in the 1950s, developed a divisional performance assessment model based on finance. By creating smaller decentralized divisions "managers could oversee from a small corporate headquarters simply by monitoring production and financial numbers."[4]

This mass production process has been adapted and used to assess system performance in education in the twenty-first century. Its application clearly distinguishes the nature and function of the educational system as industrial age. Ironically, Sloan is also associated with the concept of planned obsolescence.

Contrast these actions with the thinking of the learning organization where there is no separation between the worker and the learner. An individual must be both. All learners require a common set of core skills, attitudes, and mindsets to be successful. In the culture of the learning organization, individuals are encouraged to pursue their passions and define what they wish to be. Their commitment and loyalty is to the core purpose and functioning of the whole organization and not just one of its components. These individuals are self-managed and self-directed. The system supports them with learning programs and services to assist them in their work.

The knowledge-based society of the information age values lifelong learning, adaptation, analysis, and synthesis as well as *un-learning*. This society will be quite unforgiving of someone educated to work or learn in the industrial age paradigm. Nor will it accept someone who doesn't understand that the key to accessing quality work opportunities requires higher levels of learning and skill development than were required in the industrial age world of work. Can we continue to deal with the knowledge and learning requirements of learners in a time-driven environment of instruction built around five hours a day, one hundred and ninety days a year, and established blocks of time per subject? Reality would suggest that the answer to that question is *no*.

We need different ways to look at the problem and to do that we must also look at ourselves. We believe, at both a conscious and subconscious level, that many of the practices, procedures, and beliefs that have evolved over the past two centuries are derived from the natural order of things. They have always been with us and they are intuitive. For the most part these beliefs are not subjected to reflective thinking. They are beyond challenge because they are based on immaculate perceptions. *The penny has yet to drop.*

NOTES

1. Abraham Lincoln, Quote DB.com, www.quotedb.com/quotes/3279.
2. Daniel J. Boorstein, *The Discoverers: A History of Man's Search to Know His World and Himself* (New York: Random House, First Vintage Book Edition, 1985), 317.
3. Frederick Winslow Taylor, "Principles of Scientific Management (1911)," Marxists.org, www.marxists.org/reference/subject/economics/taylor/index.htm.
4. Michael Hammer and James Champy, *Reengineering the Corporation* (New York: HarperCollins, 1994), p. 14.

Chapter Six

Why Change? Why Now?

But this momentous question. Like a fire bell in the night, awakened and filled me with terror.[1]

Western societies have enjoyed a period of great affluence and material gain from the 1950s on. It is a time unparalleled in the annals of humankind. Paradoxically the affluence and success associated with the past six decades have contributed to our inability to grasp that our society is on the cusp of a new era. Much of what worked for us in the past will not work for us in the future. The game has changed, the rules are different, and the skills and attributes required to participate in the new paradigm differ substantially from that which we have previously known.

Edouard Balladur, former prime minister of France, expressed a concern about the increasing power and influence of Russia, China, and Islamic fundamentalists. He believes North America and Europe should form a stronger union in order to offset this growing influence. His thinking is in line with the organizing idea for the information age regarding systems interacting with systems.

He is quoted as saying that "history is starting to be made without the West and perhaps one day it will be made against it."[2] Those in North America who dismiss the attempts by China, India, and even Russia to improve or change their education systems miss the point. What they are doing, or are attempting to do, has real implications for our society on many levels.

All of us have a responsibility, in a knowledge-based society, to know, to understand, and to participate. But we are not yet a knowledge-based society despite the rhetoric to the contrary. The evolution in thinking that we need won't take place unless we collectively develop a basic understanding about what needs to change and why. As well, we need to reflect upon the models

41

of leadership that are required to create the social, economic, and political understandings about change.

This new leadership model must be able to build collaborative partnerships and develop visions and processes that would allow individuals, groups, and organizations to participate. Only through collective action and an emphasis on the common good can we ensure that these leaders properly address any societal inequities that will serve to undermine the fabric of our democratic society.

But that alone is not enough. Leaders can't lead if no one is willing to follow. If only a few people understand and are involved in the change process, then the opportunity for self-interest is greatly enhanced. That is why every citizen has a responsibility to acquire the necessary skills and insights needed to participate. The skills needed to navigate the information age or knowledge-based society are significantly different and at a higher level than those of its industrial age counterpart. Without this cognitive evolution *the gated society* will continue to be our reality.

"This time, like all times, is a very good one, if we but know what to do with it."[3] Unfortunately, we as a society do not know what to do with it.

There are no common reference points within society for initiating change of this nature. Neither is there a unifying vision that moves us in a common direction nor a mandate to begin exploring change. Likewise, significant inequities regarding access to the information, communication, and application technologies needed to create and sustain the new economy permeate our societal structures. These inequities are clearly drawn between urban and rural regions, and between rich and poor.

The issue is further complicated by a lack of informed leadership at any level of government or within any organization. We desperately need informed leadership from the business, social, professional, and volunteer ranks. These leaders must possess the will and understanding to create the thresholds for implementing the processes and developing the systems needed to support and sustain the change process. Under present circumstances we lack the systemic capacity, understanding, and processes to do what needs to be done.

What we are stuck with are organizations and systems that continue to respond to the serious issues facing us by providing what they think is needed for a society that believes it knows what it wants. We are in a time that can sustain neither of these assumptions. In the end, citizens must take a greater responsibility and exhibit a greater commitment to participation for the *greater good of all* if we are to succeed.

Many people are beginning to recognize that the *order* they have lived with is breaking down and that no viable alternative is on the horizon. The loss of jobs, the loss of homes, the loss of investment income and retirement funds, the loss of access to educational opportunities, and the loss of the middle class reinforces this view. But instead of looking to ourselves to solve our problems we continue to look to our political, economic, and social leaders to guide us. And that won't work because the knowledge, insight, and political willingness needed to lead the change we need does not exist at those levels.

How can it, when these leaders poll the population to see what we want or will accept to guide their decision making? Polls don't promote change or new thinking. They sustain the continuum of what was or is, and politicians who use this type of information to make judgments will never consider what might be. We as citizens don't collectively have the insight and knowledge to know what should be done and tend to respond to those polls based on our perceptions of the past. It is a self-evolving loop that offers little hope for change.

Rather than work together as communities around a belief of the common good, we form alliances and lobbies around specific areas of self-interest that pit one part of the community against another. We do this in order to attain personal or organizational leverage, goals, or access to resources. It is understandable why this happens. As individuals we seldom have faith that any system will treat us equitably. A large majority of us do not trust our governments. We are truly a *house divided* within and among our communities. We need leaders who understand these issues to unite and bring us together for a common purpose and a common effort.

In his inaugural address, John Kennedy appealed to the notion of the common good by saying, "Ask not what your country can do for you—ask what you can do for your country."[4] That call to action excited and engaged a whole generation of young people. But that type of thinking has now fallen by the wayside. Today, people say, "Never mind what I can do for my country; what is my country going to do for me?"

We need leaders who can capture a moment in time and engage a population in a positive dream about the future. Without some common reference points about what we should be and what we should stand for, it will be difficult to enact any meaningful change. Without that type of societal unity and purpose, the *pieces* of society will continue to sabotage or subvert the *common good* in order to ensure that the status quo is sustained. This stratification is reflected in what Warren Buffet, one of the wealthiest men in the world, is purported to have said: "There's class warfare, all right, but it's my class, the rich class, that's making war, and we're winning."[5]

Under present circumstances the political party in power throughout North America, no matter what its affiliation, seems to be more committed to the needs of the special interests that put them there, than the society in general. There is doubt and skepticism that leaders, elected or otherwise, can be advocates for the system, for individual rights, for an equitable future, or to ensure a quality way of life for all citizens. The democratic process has been hijacked and we only have ourselves to blame.

The public has little expectation that they can have any meaningful impact on any social, political, or economic issue facing the society. They have forgotten their role and responsibility in the democratic process with regard to government, institutions, and organizations. When all of us shoulder the responsibility for our circumstances then, and only then, can all of us participate in its resolution. It is too easy to take a myopic view that all of our problems are the fault of our leaders. Those leaders are merely a reflection of who we are as a society.

We need a new model of citizenship: one that recognizes the need to build new competencies and understandings in all of our citizens so that they are able to participate, work, thrive, and survive within the new paradigm. We also need to return to our obligations and responsibilities as citizens living in free societies. Creation of a new and powerful cognitive infrastructure that will inform citizenship spawns the environment in which systemic change can be properly considered.

North American towns and cities are engaged in discussions about the need to replace or renew the failing or out-of-date infrastructures for transportation, water, sewer, communication, and power. Included in that discussion should be some consideration as to how to change the processes that drive the industrial age thinking of analysis, specialization, and pieces that produced these infrastructures. That way of thinking is also an infrastructure that needs to be replaced or modified. It is worn out. As we re-create the physical infrastructure perhaps we could also re-create the cognitive infrastructure of citizenship.

Unfortunately, the necessity for working and thinking differently is not readily apparent to the vast majority of our citizens. Communities in general are attitudinally and intellectually unprepared for the realities of the twenty-first century. Given that it took the practice, form, and function of the industrial age many decades to evolve, we should be practical in our expectations about how long it will take to create something new for the information age. But we must find a starting point for the discussion.

The right leadership can create a positive culture, sustain innovation, and support initiatives for the benefit of all. The wrong leadership won't. What is needed in an information age paradigm are leaders who are not afraid to think or do, as well as people who can successfully blend the best of what is with the best of what might be. This is a time for leaders of courage and conviction, not leaders who promote system and personal compliance, the status quo, and satisfying the political need of lobbies or special interest groups. Winston Churchill suggested "that the genius of a great leader consists in the constant harmony of holding a variety of great purposes in mind all at once."[6]

These new leaders must not only understand the past, know how it has shaped the present, but also how the past and present provide insight into the future. They must help individuals, groups, and organizations map pathways to new realities. This type of leadership will not be found in organizations that have much to gain from past practice and much to fear by substantive change. The new leadership style, therefore, must be closely coupled with a renewed form of community and citizenship around alignment with information age thinking and local empowerment.

The following questions are designed to help individuals and groups reflect upon whether they have the insights and understandings to help them shift from the industrial age to the information age paradigm:

- Do I understand how the nature of work has fundamentally changed?
- Do I understand the importance of learning and how people learn in a knowledge-based economy and community?
- Have I made the personal and organizational adaptations in my practice and structures in which I work to accommodate these changes?
- Do I possess the attitudinal and intellectual framework to deal with change?
- Am I flexible, adaptable, and innovative in my practice and thinking so that I will succeed as a citizen and learner, and I will do so with excellence?
- Do I understand how current and developing technologies, especially information technologies, can be used to create or enhance new practices as well as sustain old practices that work against the new paradigm?
- Can I use technology, especially information technology, to create, develop, lead, and build partnerships, create teams, share resources, make decisions, and produce products in this new environment?
- Am I prepared for the future or am I imprisoned by my mindset of the past?

NOTES

1. Thomas Jefferson (1820), Jefferson Library at Monticello, www.monticello.org/library/reference/famquote.html.
2. Quoted in John Vinocur, "A Union of the West? Balladur Says It's Time," *International Herald Tribune*, January 7, 2008, www.iht.com/articles/2008/01/07/europe/politicus.php.
3. Ralph Waldo Emerson, QuoteWorld.org, www.quoteworld.org/quotes/4465.
4. John F. Kennedy, Inaugural Address (January 20, 1961), Bartleby.com, www.bartleby.com/124/press56.html.
5. Quoted in Ben Stein, "In Class Warfare, Guess Which Class Is Winning," *New York Times*, November 26, 2006.
6. Quoted in Steven F. Hayward, *Churchill on Leadership* (Rocklin, CA: Prima Publishing, 1997), p. xx.

Chapter Seven

The Lesson to Be Learned

Trust only movement. Life happens at the level of events, not of words.[1]

The leadership model we need in an information age environment might be that of a football team. This team combines a blend of formal and informal leadership. Who leads is determined by the circumstances on the field. Options are exercised quickly and supported through action by the rest of the team. Each individual has the skills to play a specific position and to exercise leadership when events and circumstances call upon them to lead.

The core purpose of the team is understood, as are the expectations for excellence. The coaching staff is constantly planning, analyzing, training, and assessing as a means of promoting a systems view. They emphasize continuous progress and learning by sharing, building, and creating knowledge. They build self-esteem and confidence. But as Vince Lombardi noted, "Confidence is contagious. So is the lack of confidence."[2] This could be the model upon which to base the creation of information age learning systems.

Peter Drucker observed in his book the *Post-Capitalist Society* that the historical reason for societal reform in some cultures was because the education system refused to change. He said that "rebellion against the school was the starting point for all reform movements."[3] He was referring to China and Islam but the same might hold true for us because of our public education system. Will public education be seen as a major reason why our society didn't adjust to the new paradigm and the reason why so many people are seeking alternatives to public education for their children? Or will the reform of public education, because of its connection to learning and the transmission of culture within our society, become a reason for change within our communities?

Whether our education systems can lead the reform or become the reason for the reform is a significant question. In order for public learning systems to lead reform within their communities, they must first evolve. Therein rests the paradox. In order to help reform, education systems structured around industrial age learning models must first become reformed around new models of learning. Nothing defines this need for change more dramatically than the events of September 11, 2001 (9/11). The terrible images of the terrorist attacks on the World Trade Center and the Pentagon, the tragedy of events, the senseless loss of lives, the feelings of anger, and the desire for retribution will be the hallmarks by which people recall this period of time. The attacks created a sense of vulnerability, fear, and loss within our society. Over and over again it was stated in the media that the world had changed overnight and nothing would ever be the same again. For the most part those comments were right.

It will be a topic for some time about what did change after those attacks. Eventually there will be acknowledgment that on September 11, 2001, the information age finally transcended the industrial age. The reasons why the attacks succeeded will be debated for decades. The blame will eventually be assigned to the inability of industrial age organizations to anticipate and respond to information age threats and strategies. The terrorists, although expressing beliefs and values that are hard for a Western society to comprehend, utilized Information Age practices and processes to inflict great harm on our society.

The organization of terrorism in the twenty-first century is conceived to a large degree within the context of the information age. The terrorists were able to take significant advantage of the weaknesses of an industrial age system especially when it came to the inability of individuals and groups charged with our protection and safety to build, share, and interpret knowledge.

The industrial age practice of creating organizations specializing in specific areas, like the Federal Bureau of Investigation (FBI), Central Intelligence Agency (CIA), and National Security Agency (NSA), proved to be flawed in light of these new realities. The context of the Information Age requires us to move away from a reliance on isolated areas of specialization to integrated systems thinking. This context requires new skills, new organizational structure, and new ways of working to be effective.

Although each of the organizations specializing in security and safety had critical pieces of information about what was going to happen on 9/11, they had no mechanism or predilection for sharing them with each other. In the industrial age, specialized knowledge is power and power provides access to scarce resources and influence as well as prestige. Knowledge is power in the information age as well, but only when it is shared across a system. In Industrial Age organizations there is no incentive to share what you know outside your area of specialization.

Only after the terrorists struck did those organizations try to come together to share information. The organizations designed around emergency response already do this in a superb manner. Response teams were in action immediately after the attacks. Airports and borders were closed and public officials were communicating important public messages about the events in a timely manner. These organizations were prepared and trained because they were designed to deal with accidents, tragedies, and disasters. They dealt with predictable or known outcomes. In no way, however, were the organizations charged with security and protection prepared to anticipate and respond to the events that unfolded on September 11, 2001, because something like that had never happened before.

Proactivity and prevention are not normally part of the industrial age culture. We aren't conditioned or trained to think that way. Now, many years after 9/11, we are beginning to see evidence of system integration and knowledge building as those organizations charged with our protection find new ways to fight terrorism. Perhaps it is from here that the models for the form, function, and practice of the information age will evolve.

It is ironic that the terrorists used the technological infrastructure originally designed by the Pentagon to respond to and/or prevent attacks anywhere around the globe to plan and successfully carry out their attacks. Knowing that their cell phone conversations were being monitored, the terrorists switched to the Internet as their primary method of communication. The strategic thinking employed by many people within the agencies monitoring the terrorist activities concluded that the terrorists were contained and under control. The agencies' assumptions were wrong. There is now a belief that terrorists have further adapted their practices by using Internet phone services (i.e., Voice over Internet Protocol or VOIP). These services are difficult to monitor and trace.

A significant change in Western thinking took place after 9/11. Terrorism is no longer defined as a random act of violence. It now has form and function and has been defined as a system. Once that system is understood, the powers that be can react and respond to its threats. Terrorism is now seen as an information age organization that is global, is conceptual, utilizes communication and information technology, shares information, and relies on knowledge building.

Terrorism is not an organization for good but it definitely embodies practices, procedures, and organizational structures that are aligned with information age thinking. The terrorists have built a learning organization. The events of 9/11 showed that industrial age organizations were initially unable to respond to the system of terrorism. There has been some success but it appears that most efforts are developed within the context of industrial age thinking and practice.

The attacks in Washington, D.C., and New York changed the mindset and understandings of political and business leaders, as well as members of nation-states throughout the world. It is unfortunate, but historic, that it takes a tragedy of this magnitude before such mind shifts take place. The terrorists saw an opportunity to have significant impact on the Western world by embracing a new way of doing things. They saw the vulnerabilities of a system that had failed to change or to accommodate to new realities. They saw weakness and exploited it.

In order for the alliance of Western nations to accomplish what they need to accomplish with respect to terrorism, many of our organizations will need to find ways to work and think differently. Practices, procedures, and organizational structures will have to be redefined and integrated. Knowledge building and knowledge sharing will become critical to being successful in combating terrorism. The paradigm shift has occurred, but it is not yet systemic.

World leaders are now calling for new ways of working together to ensure the sharing of information and the building of knowledge. In effect, they are giving voice to the organizing idea of the information age by requiring that systems work with systems to create and share information for the purpose of knowledge building, application, and the creation of meaning to defeat terrorism. The emphasis can longer just be on analysis of the *piece*. It must now be on analysis and then synthesis to assess the systemic implications to the organization or those organizations it is connected to.

It remains to be seen if the terrorist attacks of September 11, like the impact of Sputnik in 1957, will create the levels of urgency and understanding needed to create significant changes. So far, this has not been the case even though the lessons to be learned are in plain view. The 9/11 experiences clearly demonstrate why it is no longer acceptable to use the structures, organizations, practices, and procedures of the industrial age to meet the needs of society, the community, the world of work, and the democratic fabric of our society. The needs of the present and future cannot be met by the system of the past.

NOTES

1. Alfred Adler, quoted at Center for Academic Integrity, www.academicintegrity.org/fundamental_values_project/quotes_on_trust.php.

2. Vince Lombardi, BrainyQuote.com, www.brainyquote.com/quotes/quotes/v/vincelomba127567.html

3. Peter F. Drucker, *Post-Capitalist Society* (New York: HarperCollins, 1993), 195.

Chapter Eight

The Industrial Age
School System versus the
Information Age Learning System

The best way to predict the future is to create it.[1]

The capacities of education systems to function effectively and to initiate the changes we need within those systems have been directly impacted by the loss of local control and decision making. In most jurisdictions the centralized bureaucracy drives the educational agenda. Policy, budget, staffing formula guidelines, and union relations are in the hands of those who control the centralized agendas. Seldom are those agendas responsive to local needs and decisions.

Schools have become society's centerpiece for social, not educational, reform. If these programs are that important to society, then dollars, other than educational dollars, need to be provided to implement and sustain these initiatives. Experts should be hired who will be responsible for program implementation and the bureaucratic requirements these programs generate at both the school and district level. The school is a microcosm of the world in which it exists. Communities have transferred their social responsibilities to the school. Let teachers focus on what they have been trained to do and let communities and parents get more involved in solving problems that are rightfully theirs to solve.

Some politicians may recognize the problems and issues that face public education, but they do not seem to possess the wisdom or the will to do the right thing. This is not a new problem. General Ulysses S. Grant while with the War Department commented that government departments "are generally administered in the interest of a political party and not to serve the public interest."[2] They fail to see that their actions, their need for centralization, their social agendas, and their lack of understanding about the nature of the current change forces are responsible for limiting the capacity of the system to enact meaningful change processes.

Educational services need to be valued and treated like justice departments where government sets expectations but keep at arm's length in order for practitioners to do their jobs. By doing this, government limits the impact of political agendas. Doing this would shift the agenda for learning primarily back to the professionals in partnerships with their communities. This would mean placing the assessment of accountability and performance in the hands of the communities those professionals serve.

The loss of jobs, declining birthrates, an aging workforce, difficult working conditions, as well as other economic, political, and social issues have negatively impacted many school systems. The trend toward centralization of funding around the number of students and not the needs of the students exacerbates this problem. It serves to create a greater division between the haves and have nots, based on where you live. It is an example of proportional thinking: the industrial age axiom for the distribution of resources. It is a formula based on numbers and not need.

These concerns serve to underscore the point that the creation of educational reforms should not rest with government. Certainly government can resource the needed changes and help create new understandings among the citizenry about the need for change. But the responsibility for action should be local. Educational reform must evolve within the context of the community but under a common and collaborative set of societal reference points.

Industrial practice suggests that any change away from the status quo requires more money. The notion, however, that the provision of more money will facilitate improvement is erroneous. Arriving at conclusions about what should be reformed and why is both a cognitive and emotional challenge. Creating new understandings and a new context for education will not be easy, but it is not capital intensive. Resources will be needed to facilitate change process and to plan, develop, and create new practices and applications.

These resources will be needed to help communities to change mindsets and to create new learning organizations. Research and expertise will be needed to assist with the process, but the community and its schools must be involved in its development. The same relationships were involved during the formation of school systems in the industrial age era. Otherwise there will be no ownership of, accountability for, or understanding about what is happening or what needs to happen. Citizens need to become better informed and more knowledgeable about the world they live in so that they can apply that knowledge to the development and implementation of locally developed change processes.

"Whenever the people are well-informed they can be trusted with their own government."[3] Thoughts like these will send shudders through bureaucrats who will argue for consistency and control of both the content and the process of change. Bureaucrats will consider proposals for local control of the change process as naive and uninformed. But one only has to consider what bureaucrats of education have done, or not done, with their opportunity to change the system over the past two decades to gain some comfort with this new direction. These bureaucrats have a role to play but their involvement should be controlled and restricted. Let them resource and manage the changes and help formulate a process for support and common direction but don't let them set the agenda. If they do the agenda will be self-serving, incompetent, top down, and designed to fail.

One of the first questions to be considered in this change process concerns the focus of public education. Should it stay on liberal arts or shift toward preparation for the workplace? Or does the emphasis fit somewhere in between as we redefine the role of citizenship, the role of learning, and the new requirements for citizenship in the twenty-first century? These are the types of questions that need discussion and resolution before moving forward.

We also need to be mindful that the call to initiate and move forward with reform can mean different things to different people, depending on their perspective and their experience. That is why a clear definition, understanding, and consensus as to what is to be achieved are needed before the reform process can begin.

Because of the preponderance of industrial age thinkers in leadership and governance positions, the concept of reform will be resisted. It will also be resisted by local agents and representatives of the centralized authority. Communities must gain the critical mass and understanding to overcome this resistance. In doing so, reform leaders must try to capture the imagination of communities, elicit support and partnerships both within and without the education system, and create a positive sense of the future.

Understandings that will serve as touchstones for moving forward to attain these goals are as follows:

- The primary concern of the change initiative is to create, maintain, and/or sustain learning environments that promote success in terms of the intellectual, social, and emotional development of learners.
- No aspect of the organization should be excluded from the discussion. There can be no *sacred cows* when considering change.
- The solution for effective and sustainable change resides with the creation of a new learning organization within the context of community around the new realities created by the information age paradigm. Fixing the old organization will not be productive.
- Every part of the organization is connected. This will require a rethink of many things including administrative practices, governance, organizational procedures, facilities, and technology required to support quality-learning environments.

- The change initiative should be designed to capture the imagination of communities, build consensus, hope, and partnerships, as well as promote a positive view toward dealing with change in a difficult and complex environment.
- The function, form, structure, and purpose of a public learning organization are designed around what we know about learning and how people learn. Not only will this knowledge impact on instructional practices but also it will impact on leadership, communication, work environments, and partnerships with other systems.
- The primary purpose of the change initiative is to position the public learning system to survive and thrive in the new millennium and to link it strategically to other systems that support learners.
- We must be sure to develop a systems approach that is aligned with the practice of the information age and not industrial age thinking.
- A relevant and competent Information Age learning system is a key subset for economic, social, and political renewal.

Whether we have the will and resolve to do what is needed is a question that can't be answered at this time. History will determine whether we have the collective wisdom to change our learning systems so that all of us have the opportunity to adjust, adopt, and adapt to new realities.

Some countries in Europe appear to have begun the complex process of finding ways to strengthen communities and renew their education systems in response to the challenges of creating a culture aligned with the new paradigm. As useful as many of the institutions and organizations of the past have been for Western Europeans and North Americans, they are not likely to be functional in the future world. We are at a point in time that is neither well defined nor clearly understood.

"He was," Matthew Arnold might have said, "wandering between two worlds, one dead, the other powerless to be born."[4] "He" refers to Danish astronomer Tycho Brahe. This quotation could also serve to describe the mismatch between the industrial age and the information age. The new paradigm represented by the emergence of the information age is at times lost and struggling to find form and substance whereas the industrial age is very much with us in our personal and organizational beliefs and practices.

Learning and how people learn is the only unifying element at this time that is common to all of us. The world lying ahead of us is one that requires human invention, creativity, and innovation in almost every sphere of action and endeavor. For this to happen we cannot afford to waste any human intelligence.

If this book succeeds, it will create a tangible vision for what a public learning system might look and feel like as well as how it would work on a day-to-day basis. What is being proposed is a working design for creating change. This design is far from complete. It is intended to stimulate thinking and discussion, and to support others in that process.

Part of that stimulation and discussion can be aided by looking at education and learning through the lens of each paradigm. Table 8.1 highlights the distinctions between the two systems. These distinctions lay the groundwork for redesigning our current system. The industrial age list defines the form, function, and practice of the present and past. The information age list defines the form, function, and practice of the future.

Table 8.1. Contrasts between Industrial Age Education and Information Age Learning Systems

Public Education System	Public Learning System
Focus on teaching and instruction.	Focus on learning and how people learn.
Focus on replication of society.	Greater emphasis on the transformation and reinvention of society.
Assumption that learning is for the young.	Learning is an essential life skill that continues throughout life.
Differentiation between those who work and those who learn.	Learners must be workers and workers must be learners.
Teaching based on content specialty.	Teaching bridges content and processes of learning (integration).
Learning is fragmented, specialized, and generally abstract.	Learning is directly connected to knowledge building and application.
Leadership emanates from content expertise.	Leadership emanates from expertise on learning and how people learn (process and content).
Organization constructed around components of education (pieces equal the whole—fragmentation).	Organization built around concepts of learning (systems interacting with systems).
Schooling isolated from community— defined around thirteen segments from kindergarten to grade twelve.	Learning defined within a systems environment (integrated systems) as part of community (lifelong learning).
Focus on average for group.	Focus on individual ability.
Assessment of group performance for accountability.	Assessment of individual and group performance for accountability and development of learning plans.
Planning seen as an isolated, external event (does not promote organization, consistency, or coherency).	Planning seen as an integral, ongoing part of keeping the learning system coherent, consistent, and relevant.
Technology used to enhance organizational fragmentation.	Technology used to integrate knowledge— maintain systems focus.
Technology provides digitized content as defined by common industrial age curriculum.	Technology provides information/resources to support quality learning and learning outcomes based on learners' preferences.

(continued)

Table 8.1. (*Continued*)

Public Education System	Public Learning System
Collaboration to review and modify one piece of the whole.	Collaboration to build and share knowledge in the system around its core activity.
Known primarily by what you do (content).	Known by what you do (content) and how you do it (process).
Service provider determines what you need and when you get it.	Clients determine what they want and when they need it (anytime, anyplace, anywhere, anypace, anyone).
People within organization determine/assess your potential.	Individual learner determines own potential through demonstrated performance.
Organizational culture is composite of distinctive organizational specialties (math, science, library).	Organizational culture reflects commonality determined by learning, knowledge building, and knowledge sharing, no matter what area of specialization is involved.
System is separate from its community.	System is integrated into its community.
System emulates practice, organization, and function of organizations and institutions.	System helps community and organizations develop new practice, organization, and function.

NOTES

1. Peter F. Drucker, What Quote.com, www.whatquote.com/quotes/Peter-F—Drucker/31616-The-best-way-to-pred.htm.

2. Quoted in Jean Edward Smith, *Grant* (New York: Simon & Schuster, 2001), 460.

3. Thomas Jefferson, quoted at University of Virginia Library etext, etext.virginia.edu/jefferson/quotations/jeff1350.htm.

4. Quoted in Daniel J. Boorstein, *The Discoverers: A History of Man's Search to Know His World and Himself* (New York: Random House, First Vintage Book Edition, 1985), 307.

Chapter Nine

Planning to Plan—How to Create Systemic Change Consistent with Information Age Thinking

There is nothing more difficult to take in hand, more perilous to conduct, or more uncertain in its success, than to take the lead in the introduction of a new order of things.[1]

Developing an accurate diagnosis of the problem, whether it is medical or otherwise, is the starting point for any action. Arriving at a cure or a solution based on that diagnosis is a far greater challenge. The following processes and comments are intended to provide a structure for developing the diagnosis as well as suggest some possible cures and/or solutions for creating an information age learning system.

A beginning point for this discussion can be found in the research on learning and how people learn. *How People Learn: Bridging Research and Practice* provides an excellent introduction to this research.[2] A fundamental premise of *The Gated Society* is that the research on learning provides both a rationale and an insight as to how we should reform our education system.

One of the first constructs of effective teaching is to ensure that the learner has the correct information or prior learning upon which to build new learning. Industrial thinking and practice have shaped our existing societies' prior learning. But it is no longer the correct learning upon which to base change initiatives or processes for our future. It follows then that professionals and community members must first query and validate both their personal and organizational prior learning before they can participate in any discussion about change or reform.

It has been previously stated that the organizing idea for the industrial age is structured around reducing a body of knowledge into component pieces, studying that knowledge, and developing areas of specialization around those distinct and unique bodies of information. The emphasis is on analysis and the assumption is that an aggregation of the pieces equals the whole. Industrial age thinking and practice, the shape of organizations, and their function within society are designed around this idea. Strategic planning models used by industrial age organizations and institutions are based on this same type of thinking. The information age is about systems interacting or converging with other systems to create knowledge, meaning, and application. Learning, and how people learn, is a key component of its infrastructure. It is an infrastructure designed to build, share, acquire, develop, apply, and sometimes, reinvent knowledge. Both analysis and synthesis are important.

This means that the thinking and practice that guides the function and form of information age organizations must be different from industrial age thinking and practice. A systemic knowledge-based planning model is a key resource or tool for creating change, involving community, and incorporating new thinking and practice. The strategic planning model based on an industrial age way of thinking is outdated and of no value in this context.

The new planning model embraces the organizing concepts of the information age—knowledge, learning, systems, analysis, and synthesis. Simply restructuring or transforming industrial age organizing concepts as a means of enabling information age organizing concepts cannot work. The two organizing ideas are not compatible or interchangeable.

In other words, the components of a new learning system must be derived from the information age paradigm and must be understood by all those who participate in the change process. As well, the systemic or knowledge-based planning model that is used must provide systems, organizations, or communities with a process by which they can structure change initiatives geared specifically to the information age. The research on learning and how people learn provides insight as to the shape and form of this new planning model as well as to the content and nature of the change. The prior learning for creating an information age learning system can't be an extension of industrial age thinking and practice.

The component pieces that comprise the new learning system may be similar in name and general purpose to their industrial age counterparts, but they serve a different purpose. These new components interact with each other in a different manner because they are cast within an Information Age context. A review of the websites for school boards, superintendents, principals, curriculum and supervision, and teachers' unions underscores this point.

Each site references its area of specialization and outlines its ideas for reforms or changes based on that specialization. These sites do not recognize or acknowledge the other components of the organization in their web overviews. Each component works as an entity unto itself. There is no recognition in their thinking that it takes the combined and integrated effort of all the areas of specialization to achieve any measurable change. Each piece sees what it does as being the most important to the organization. Any initiative they put forward therefore, lacks the capacity to create or sustain systemic change because of the singular focus.

The National Association of Secondary School Principals (NASSP) is about promoting excellence in middle and high school leadership. The National School Board Association (NSBA) aims to foster excellence and equity in public schools through school board leadership. The Association for Supervision and Curriculum Development (ASCD) promotes sound policies and best practices to achieve the success of each learner. The American Association of School Administrators (AASA) focuses on strong school system leadership to improve lives of children. And the National Education Association (NEA) believes in great public schools for each child.

These websites promote change and excellence but they do so from their area of specialization. These sites do not promote a systemic perspective about the changes the other *pieces of the organization* must make in order for the reform to succeed. Instead the change they envision for their area of specialization, often a transformative and not a transcending view, is perceived transferable to all other areas of the system. It is a narrow perspective of organizational change.

How then can there be a systemic reform if the pieces that represent the system lack the collective ability to work together to create a context for change? The answer rests in the creation of a new planning model because the existing planning model lacks the capacity to do this. What is needed is a model that:

- Provides information about the research on learning and about the change process in the new paradigm.
- Promotes consideration of a systemic transition strategy that allows and supports a migration from an industrial to an information age organization.
- Utilizes, interprets, and makes decisions based on knowledge-driven data.
- Develops an expectation that all of the pieces that constitute and support the system must work together around the common good if the systemic process is to be successful.
- Creates an understanding of how the clients of the system (specifically) and society (in general) will benefit from the change (i.e., how the changes to organizational function, form, and practice are relevant to the world of work, the quality of life, and to the well-being of the community).
- Demonstrates the commonality that the pieces share and develops processes and expectations for information sharing, knowledge acquisition, knowledge integration, knowledge building, learning, and unlearning.
- It is ongoing and not periodic so that the organization can shift, change, or adjust in a timely and relevant manner.

The political, economic, and social readiness needed to initiate and implement this new planning model is considerable. Creating a new organization *on the fly*, so to speak, is complex, challenging, and fraught with difficulties, but there seems to be no other alternative if the goal is to look for an orderly and thoughtful transition from one paradigm to another. It does not seem possible or realistic to bring one system to a halt and begin another. Historically, this does not tend to happen unless the *old* system is totally destroyed by social, political, or economic events. Will our willingness to work on this collectively help us avoid that outcome? Are we able to learn to change and then change to learn? Only time will tell.

Learning, and how we learn, is key to making the knowledge-based planning model work. Dr. Milt McClaren, working with Royal Roads University in Victoria, British Columbia, has succinctly summarized the research on learning. His three main classifications or generalizations about learning theory follow:

1. Prior knowledge exerts an important influence on new learning.
2. Competence in a field requires both a deep foundation of factual knowledge, an understanding of the facts in the context of a conceptual framework, and knowledge organized in ways that facilitates retrieval and application.
3. Instruction that pays explicit attention to learners' metacognitive capacities can help learners develop the ability to select and apply appropriate learning tactics and monitor their application and effectiveness.[3]

These generalizations provide the framework for systemic change. They create a context for the development of learning environments, as well as insight into the organizational practice, form, and function needed to sustain these environments. They suggest changes to instructional practices and curriculum experiences as well as to the structures and procedures of the organization that support those practices and experiences.

They also have significant implications with regard to the changes we need to make with respect to organizational components or pieces such as governance, leadership, teaching, curriculum, assessment practices, collaboration, and the use of technology, teams, and partnerships. To achieve this we must also develop new models of cooperation and collaboration recognizing that there may be more agreement regarding the process of change than there will be on the content of change. All of these are important considerations in the planning process.

This new planning model begins with an assumption that the basic unit of change in the information age is the individual mind. Therefore, the first generalization regarding prior learning has to be the starting point for change. Changing individual mindsets, through learning and knowledge building, is the trigger for initiating organizational change. It requires all of those who participate in change process to be knowledgeable about change and to be vigilant about the paradoxes that may exist within themselves between what they know and what they feel.

Mental models need to be developed that help individuals understand and monitor their words, beliefs, perceptions, assumptions, and actions. What people believe and agree to intellectually may not match the reality of their practice. The former is derived from conscious thought and vetted by logic. The latter is fashioned from experience and is replicated in the form of patterned and instinctive behavior housed within the subconscious mind.

These behaviors are sometimes fashioned from the assumptions and perceptions developed within an emotional circumstance and have more to do with feeling than fact. They can both hinder or support the change process. The expression "I hear what you say but I am going to watch the way your feet move" serves as a good reference point for action.

Developing new models for thinking around these generalizations may mean that we have to consider changing that with which we are most comfortable or that which has brought us the most personal and organizational success. If an individual's or an organization's prior learning is not accurate or relevant, it cannot be an appropriate base upon which to construct new learning, knowledge, meaning, and application.

The first generalization is about being prepared mentally to participate in the planning process. The second generalization put forth by Dr. McClaren provides the impetus for the bulk of the planning. This generalization helps us understand what knowledge and insights we need to acquire or develop as we explore the pieces that make up the organization we wish to change. To do this requires participants to have an understanding of the area of specialization under review as well as to possess the knowledge or content needed to create transition, understanding, and transfer. Planners must be able to integrate these understandings into the key concepts or major frameworks by which meaning and application can be developed.

Accommodating this second generalization readies members of the planning process to engage in the third generalization of the learning process and that is planning for new learning. It is at this point that participants in the planning process are able to design, develop, and implement the components of the public learning system based on their review of the pieces. The learning system becomes a sustainable reality and the ongoing planning process promotes continuous improvement and excellence.

NOTES

1. Niccolo Machiavelli, BrainyQuote.com, www.brainyquote.com/quotes/quotes/n/niccolomac131418.html.

2. National Academy of Sciences, Summary, *How People Learn: Bridging Research and Practice,* M. Suzanne Donovan, John D. Bransford, and James W. Pellegrino, eds. (Washington, D.C.: National Academy Press, 1999), www.nap.edu/html/howpeople2/notice.html.

3. Milton McClaren, "EECO Week 3. Design for Learning. The Challenges and Opportunities of Human Diversity in the Design of Learning Environments" (course notes, Royal Roads University, Victoria, B.C., 2007).

Chapter Ten

Prior Learning—Assumptions, Perceptions, and Presumptions (Generalization One)

Democracy cannot succeed unless those who express their choice are prepared to choose wisely. The real safeguard of democracy, therefore, is education.[1]

Biographies often tell stories about how individuals achieved levels of excellence that no one ever expected of them. Peers are surprised at the success or the accomplishments of these individuals. Their talents and abilities were sometimes hidden from view. That is because many people do not readily display to others what they know or what they don't know. Nor do they always openly share their passionate views or beliefs on a topic until time and circumstances require it of them. The external face people often put forward does not always reflect what the internal self knows or believes. Therefore, when we govern, lead, or plan, we must be careful not to trust our assumptions about other people's abilities, talents, or understanding of an issue.

The research on learning and how people learn requires those charged with instruction to assess a learner's prior learning to ensure that it is correct and not faulty or filled with errors. This is not something that is done very well across the system in public or postsecondary education. The nature of the organization fosters the practice, more often than not, of whole group instruction and teaching *to the middle*. The classroom logistics of individually assessing prior learning on an ongoing basis on any given learning outcome are significant. Under present circumstances and time constraints it is difficult, if not impossible, to do.

Classrooms are one concern. What about communities and organizations that serve the community? The prior learning that many people have may be relevant only to their past. With the changing circumstances precipitated by the emergence of the information age, that prior learning may have little application or value.

This reality imposes significant challenges in terms of trying to change the instructional process, reform the education system, or reinvent a community. This is not to say that all information/knowledge from the industrial age is wrong. It's not, but the context in which it exists has changed. There is an abundance of new knowledge to displace old knowledge and it is happening at a faster rate than most of us can sustain. Instead of relying on a continuum of facts, apart from those that compose the new basics, we need to rely on processes for finding and validating information. Therefore, the process of assessing prior learning and determining which paradigm it represents becomes more critical.

The following statements are examples of how faulty and misleading some assumptions can be. These statements are examples of prior learning that guide practice in some classrooms but which are not substantiated by research.

1. *Education systems must restore educational standards by putting a new emphasis on the old basics and establishing standards equivalent to those of previous years.* Many of the *old basics* are content based such as reading, writing, and arithmetic. They are important but, in today's world, so are technical reading and writing and the sciences, especially genetics, mathematics, and technology. Equally important are the process skills for thinking, learning, and communicating, including the abilities for problem solving, critical thinking analysis, and synthesis. Suggesting that education systems go back to the basics reflects a narrow and limiting view that will not serve the need of learners in a twenty-first-century society.

2. *Top-down change never works. Only change coming from the bottom up can work.* Leadership is necessary to create, articulate, and implement a vision of what should be. Leaders have the formal authority to allocate resources, create and enforce mandates, and to supervise. This is critical to the success of any change or implementation. Those at the bottom part of the hierarchy tend not to have a holistic view of the whole organization. They are specialists and have a lot of knowledge and information about a specific part of the organization. But without their involvement, support, and contribution, any change process has little chance of succeeding. Everyone in the organization has to be involved and *believe together* if the initiative is going to work. Top down and bottom up are more about who has power than it is about a description of an effective work and learning environment. This hierarchy of power has been responsible for the inability of industrial age organizations to ever make or create substantial change together. The process is usually top down and implemented at the expense of those on the lower rungs of the employment ladder. In the knowledge-based system both top and bottom will be united and structured around the expertise of learners to support the common

good. The use of the pyramid to represent the system will no longer be valid. The relationship, driven by learning, might best be represented by a circle.

3. *The pace of change needs to be slowed.* This comment is reflective of the monopolistic view that people at all levels in the education system have toward change. They believe that any change process is within the control of the organization to shape how, when, where, and why change takes place. It is a view that recognizes and acknowledges the power of various special interest groups within that structure to establish the parameters for any change process both in terms of content and pace. It is unrealistic and isolationist. Meanwhile, the world external to the system is forced to thrive and survive in an environment of rapid and unrelenting change. This unrealistic balance between the two impedes the changes that are necessary to keep public education aligned with the world in which it exists. The experience of other organizations that have suffered and failed from this type of thinking should be a warning to those in public education. Practitioners within the education organization will become marginalized and insignificant if they don't change, and change quickly.

4. *Change is dependent on more money, resources, and staffing.* The proper resource and support of any change process is needed if it is to be successful. In today's world, it is unlikely that any large infusions of cash will be provided to education systems to support change initiatives. The real change must first take place within the thinking and understanding that people have about what needs to change and why. This type of change is not capital intensive. There is a lot of money spent on educational organizations but seldom are new practices and/or new organizational structures considered as a means of creating efficiencies. That would require the system to undo or unlearn what it normally does. There are no formal processes or practices in place within school systems to think and plan in this manner. That doesn't mean it can't be done. Once there is an understanding about what needs to change, some of the money and resources needed can be found within the existing structure by utilizing a business reengineering process. This process can help people see what practices and structures are no longer relevant as well as reveal new and more efficient ways to achieve the same results.

5. *The socioeconomic background of the student and social problems of society prevent teachers from being successful with some students.* Good citizenship is part of any classroom environment. But the implementation of a wide variety of social/political programs is interfering with the core purpose of the learning system and the opportunities for teachers to teach. Communities and families need to reassume their responsibilities and get over the idea that harassment, drugs, smoking, and violence only take place during the time kids are in school. As well, governments need to do their accountability and

achievement assessments in a manner that does not burden the school nor control, limit, and direct the learning agenda for students. And, practitioners need to quit explaining poor achievement as a product of social circumstances. Parents can play an important role in the readiness a child has for learning when they arrive at school. Under present circumstances it defaults to the teacher and the school to make the difference, and they can with the right practice and support. But the social and economic circumstances of learners should not be a reason for lower expectations about their ability or willingness to learn.

6. *Kids learn best sitting in straight rows, being quiet, and, "taking on all the attributes of dead people."* This is not how learning, exploration, application, and discovery take place. Order and respect are important, and the teacher must have control in order to manage the learning environment, but the teacher must be very knowledgeable about learning and how people learn. The research says that learning should be managed within an environment of problem solving, working in teams, demonstrating and employing real-world applications, knowledge building, and creativity. Sitting quietly in rows works well when the teacher is master of all knowledge and the learners' job is to regurgitate only what was taught. That was the practice that guided the learning in the industrial age classrooms of previous decades. It is not the practice that will serve learners well, both in the present and the future.

7. *Kids who answer the question first are the smartest and brightest.* We know that some learners reflect upon a question for five to ten seconds before they develop and confirm an answer. Even when they have an answer, they may decide not to share it with anyone else. A teacher, therefore, who poses a question and then takes an answer from those who put their hands up first is doing a disservice to the process of learning. On one hand, it negates the thinking process of the reflective learner. On the other, it allows the rest of the class to disengage from learning related to that particular question. It is better for a teacher to create a healthy expectation that everyone is able to, and will, learn. Effective practice creates an expectation that every learner is expected to answer the question, provides time for learners to engage in thinking about an answer, and provides an opportunity for a student who doesn't get the right response to go back, research, and come up with the right answer. Classroom practices like this support learners' self-esteem, create opportunities for success, and engage people in the learning process.

8. *Learners learn best when concepts are taught in sequence from the simplistic to the complex.* Not all learning is linear or sequential. Some students skip various stages of problem solving, focus on the more complex issues, and come back to the more simplistic aspects of the question. Progress occurs as learners put the problem into a context that they can understand. Teachers

must be aware of how students learn and accommodate a variety of thinking processes when learners are seeking a solution to a problem.

9. *Kids who don't pay attention in class have an attitude problem, don't want to learn, and will never succeed.* This response is subjective. Schools are faced with some significant behavioral problems from some students but that has always been true. Some of these problems are caused by classroom practice. If teachers are so *lock-step* in their thinking and unimaginative in their teaching that learners become bored, then behavioral problems will surface. Bored students soon become disruptive students.

Successful teachers feel that it is their responsibility to engage all learners in the classroom. They try to create expectations that everyone will participate and will succeed with the concepts being taught. It isn't left up to a learner to decide whether he or she is going to work or not work. This approach isn't always successful, but it is more proactive and engages more learners than that of a teacher who says, "I have taught it and it is up to you as a learner to learn it." Sometimes a visit to a skateboard park will demonstrate a model of learning that is not always seen in schools. Some of the participants you will see are viewed as nonlearners and behavior problems in their schools. At the skateboard park they can be seen mastering difficult and complex maneuvers on skateboards. They are working and learning within a multiaged group of people who share a similar passion. They nurture each other's self-esteem and support each other in developing skills, understanding, and applications. They encourage risk taking and collectively set high but appropriate standards for performance. They aspire to excellence in what they do and achieve. They engage in the learning process because the elements of a good learning and instructional environment are available—elements they couldn't find in their classrooms.

10. *Learning is best served by a content-based curriculum, standards, a focus on traditional basic skills, accountability, written assessments, a five-hour day, a one-hundred-and-ninety-day school year, and by teaching to the average in a classroom.* These descriptors describe most public education systems in North America as well as the expectations many parents have for schooling. But it is an educational design that is no longer relevant or functional given today's societal needs. It is a model strongly influenced by our agrarian past and sustained by our industrial age practice. Why do we sustain this model when we know it is no longer appropriate? There is not enough time in the present structure of the instructional day or the year to teach and to learn that which is most important to working, learning, and citizenship in this new age. Teachers need time and flexibility to pursue different learning venues when an *aha* moment occurs with a student. But the politics of trying to change any aspect of the present arrangement are prohibitive.

11. *Leaders within our public education systems have the skills and insights to create, manage, and implement the changes that are needed to make education systems relevant, competent, and in tune with new realities.* Not true. There are people both within and outside the system who are trying to create substantive change but most of today's change agenda is driven by notions of accountability, achievement, standards, and back to the basics. In reality most leaders in the educational community where these notions are in play have been forced into *system compliance.* The centralized authority demands it. Innovation and creativity at the local level have been stifled in favor of participation in the one overarching or central view of what an education system should be. The people, or persons, who have the bureaucratic or political control of the system usually promote this view. They control both the processes and the content of the system and ignore the expertise, advice, and contribution of those closest to the action. This type of leadership is arrogant, egotistical, and prone to political favoritism and motivation. It conjures up practice that is contrary to any of the literature on management and leadership about creating competent organizations or assessing their performance.

12. *Teachers will lead us to new levels of reform.* The suggestion that teachers as individuals will keep up to date with research and adopt and adapt new practices on a systemwide basis is an erroneous one. If there is no *healthy anxiety* or leadership within the system to create this expectation, then most people opt for the practice and procedures that have sustained them in the past. Because teachers are specialists they generally lack a systems view about the organization they work in and seldom have access to the resources or processes needed to direct and manage change. If one person creates a meaningful innovation at the classroom level, there are few formal mechanisms to leverage or communicate that change so that the whole system benefits from the newfound expertise or knowledge.

13. *Principals will lead us to new levels of reform.* Many principals focus on their own schools and their needs. They prefer to work individually and not in concert with other schools. As with teachers, principals have limited access to resources and decision making to implement and sustain systemic change. They deal primarily with their site because that is the practice promoted within industrial age organizations. This type of leadership model is competitive and it pits one school against another in terms of performance, both academically and athletically. Those who excel are rewarded. Therefore, principals tend to be engaged in the things that they can influence within their own buildings and are generally concerned with the whole system.

14. *Universities are in the best position to train teachers and create leaders to work in an information age school system.* A review of some university

websites revealed a desire on the part of many department faculties to shift instructional practices to emphasize problem solving and incorporate real-world applications of learning into the classroom experience. This shift in thinking and practice was not reflected in the faculties of education at those universities. The experience and training a new teacher received in those institutions did not appear to vary significantly from past practice. This review was by no means comprehensive but it serves as a reminder that any change within the system, especially pertaining to learning and instruction, has to involve postsecondary institutions—not as leaders of, but as partners in, what needs to change.

15. *Boys and girls learn the same, but girls have a better attitude toward learning.* Boys in North America are not being as successful as they should be. The system has done well over the past two decades to respond to the learning needs of girls and must make a similar commitment for boys. Boys have different interests than girls and they learn differently. Accommodations need to be made in instructional processes, expectations, curriculum, and library resources as a means of promoting their success with learning.

16. *Mastery of a concept is not important before moving on to the next concept.* Because of issues of time in the classroom and the demands of provincial or state exams, many teachers follow a practice where concepts are presented and then the teacher moves on. If the learner doesn't get it, then it's generally up to the learner to seek extra help. This practice is contrary to the Principles of Learning followed by the Ministry of Education, British Columbia.[2] Learners learn at different speeds and in different ways. Teachers know this and believe in this, but cannot adequately address this reality within the structure and expectations of the industrial age classroom. Classroom practice is constrained because of requirements to cover the content. This forces teachers to teach to the average or the middle. There is not enough time to stop and explore different ideas or concepts as they arise. Because of these constraints, teachers, not learners, set the rate of learning in the classroom.

17. *The most important aspect of learning is to be able to recall basic information for a test.* Standardized exams include questions of analysis, synthesis, and application, but it is not expected that all or most students will successfully meet this expectation for testing. Most tests, related to government standards, and classroom expectations are still designed around recall. This means that the standard of assessment is still built and designed around low expectations for performance. If the tests were really designed around what students need to master and be able to demonstrate and do in a twenty-first-century environment, the results would prove embarrassing to both governments and school districts.

18. *Not everyone can learn math.* Being unable to learn math has more to do with teaching than it does with learning. It is not uncommon to hear parents say, "I wasn't any good at math either" and provide acceptance and understanding for those children who don't do well with this subject. Acknowledging poor performance in math is socially acceptable within our communities. Interesting enough, it would not be the same for reading. Most people would be embarrassed to acknowledge that they cannot read. How well they can read is a different question. We need to create the same expectation we have for reading around math. It is one of the fundamental and basic skills required to properly function in a technical world. We know what needs to change in the instructional processes to help more learners be successful, but it seems to be difficult to reshape classroom practice across our systems to accommodate these changes.

19. *Human performance falls within a bell curve.* The use of the term *bell curve* has become unpopular, but when you look at provincial, state, and international assessments, or when you look at university entrance and scholarship exams, you realize that it is very much in place. Administrators have just found different ways, through statistical management, to ensure that the top 10 or 15 percent of students are on the plus side of the curve. There is no place for mastery learning in this process.

These unfounded assumptions about learning that guide present practices don't just exist in our schools; they also exist in our communities. These community assumptions, although not supported by research, help to shape and sustain some practices that guide learning in our schools. Some of those community assumptions are as follows:

- *My son or daughter is going to university.* At grade eight, a large majority of parents, and students, would list this as an outcome of a secondary education. It speaks to their dreams and hopes for their children. The percentage of those who go on to postsecondary education in actuality is much smaller. More effort needs to be made at the grade seven and eight levels to educate parents and students about the value of a career in technology and trades. It should not be viewed as a *less than* option compared to university. If community expectations and support for these technology programs were higher, then we might see more of them in our schools.
- *An A is the best indicator of achievement.* People understand the value of an A based on their own experience with public education. Generally an A is still earned in school by doing things the same way as when adults were students. The problem is that an A seldom includes an assessment of some of the *new skills* like problem solving, teamwork, or real-world application

of knowledge. We need to find a better assessment model of achievement. A lot of work has been done in this area, but the new models of assessment being proposed won't work unless the instructional model also changes.

• *We need to return to basics and standards.* Parents generally want the education that they received to be replicated for their children. It's what made them successful. There is a general awareness that we are in new times, but there is little reflection upon what that means in terms of the skills and experiences children should receive in school.

• *The best classroom is quiet and orderly.* Parents are used to, and generally are comfortable with, the stand and deliver model of instruction of the industrial age era. They associate quiet with order. The models of instruction that support individual learning application and demonstration are not often seen, understood, or appreciated, with the exception perhaps of primary classrooms.

• *We don't have high expectations for the school because we live in a rural area.* Parents have a belief that educational opportunities and standards are lower in rural areas. Perhaps they are right. They don't have the same expectations for performance today that they had in previous times. Yet for much of our history, an education in a rural school prepared many learners for access to postsecondary institutions. Being rural didn't mean that your educational options were second class and less than what your urban counterparts would receive. Funding programs that focus on the number of students and space being utilized make it substantially more difficult to deliver adequate programs to rural and remote areas.

• *Lots of homework is indicative of high classroom expectations.* Parents think that homework is synonymous with diligence, a willingness to learn, and high classroom expectations. They do not understand that homework is sometimes given because there is not enough time in the classroom to cover material. If the homework is used to practice or extend learning from the classroom, then it is good. When it is used to expose a learner to new learning on his or her own, without a context, then it is unacceptable. The statement "we have met the enemy and he is us"[3] is quite appropriate in this situation.

These examples of organizational and individual assumptions, perceptions, and presumptions that inform our prior learning and keep us from changing are what we need to change in education. They also keep us divided at a time when we need unity of purpose and consistency of action. Our beliefs should not limit our opportunities to learn, to adapt, and to change. This also holds true for the world of work, citizenship, personal and organizational performance, and community participation.

The following example demonstrates how a belief can become institutionalized and no longer vetted by conscious thought. A presenter at a conference on secondary reform (name and location long forgotten) used the following example to demonstrate an organizational assumption that guided current practice even though it evolved from a previous century. The presenter noted that room lighting generally found in schools runs parallel to the window wall. This architectural practice evolved from agrarian times because of the placement of blackboards and the early dependence on natural light. He wanted to turn the lights off at the front of the room to enhance his power-point presentation but couldn't because of the lighting design.

Although we were in a modern facility for the presentation, the lighting was arranged in the same way. It was a design feature influenced by an assumption on prior learning that was over one hundred years old. It is the way it has always been done and no one was bothering to question why. When we think about prior learning we usually think about an individual. We normally don't think about the organizational intelligence or prior learning housed in the collective mindsets of practitioners. Doing so will open up new ideas and understandings about what needs to change.

This understanding can be achieved by reflecting on the individual and organizational prior learning that guides the design of schools, the organization of districts, and the practices, procedures, organizational culture, and functions that apply to instruction, leadership, governance, learning, use of technology, program delivery, and services. Asking ourselves if this prior learning is correct or valid is the starting point for action or change.

NOTES

1. Franklin D. Roosevelt, enotes.com, www.enotes.com/famous-quotes/democracy-cannot-succeed-unless-those-who-express.

2. Ministry of Education, British Columbia, "Principles of Learning," September 2000, www.bced.gov.bc.ca/resourcedocs/k12educationplan/k12program/k12prog_02.htm.

3. Walt Kelly (1972), www.igopogo.com/we_have_met.htm.

Chapter Eleven

Defining the Philosophical Thrust and Structure of the Learning Organization (Generalization Two)

Don't serve what is. Our job is to serve what might be.[1]

The second generalization of learning theory provided by Dr. Milton Mc-Claren provides the opportunity to develop new organizational practice, form, and function. This opportunity is comprised of two parts. The first part provides the guidelines or touchstones for creation, design, and development. The second part is the product or outcome generated by using those touchstones or guidelines.

Part one begins with the creation of a vision that defines the philosophical thrust and structure of the organization to be created. Part two establishes a new context for, and the development of, a site-system relationship. Together, they clarify how the system will work or function.

PART ONE: CREATING THE VISION

The vision for a new learning system evolves from an understanding of learning, the importance of knowledge and knowledge building to organizations, and from a thorough knowledge of the two paradigms. Planners need to be conversant with how the industrial and information age paradigms are alike and how they are different. The vision gives a philosophical purpose and direction to all other activities and enables action within the organization or institution.

The vision has to address the current economical, social, and political realities of the community, has to relate to the core business or purpose of the enterprise or organization, and should be clear, concise, and memorable. Vision statements that are all-encompassing, wordy, and/or vague produce organizations with similar characteristics. Creating an informed vision statement is the first task in defining an organizational structure. In a knowledge-based society, a vision can be the work or perspective of one individual but it cannot serve as the vision of the organization unless it is validated and owned by others in the organization.

Industrial age organizations bring representative groups together to create a vision statement and then set about to create compliance throughout the whole organization around the announced statement. It is the basis for their *strategic* plans. Learning organizations on the other hand must be more open and proactive. The vision statement could be the work of an individual, but it must be vetted and confirmed before being proclaimed.

These organizations must unite all of the people in the organization around the vision statement if they wish to have any success with the change agenda. This statement should be an integral and daily reference point for all members of the organization regarding the organizational practice, function, and form. It serves as a constant beacon for excellence, change, relevance, and passion.

A vision statement that anticipates the structure and needs of a learning organization and the individuals within it will facilitate change. It must embrace learning and how people learn. It will serve as a guidepost for aligning organizational activities that empower people to apply their creativity and expertise toward attainment of the core purpose of the organization. It will also encourage thinking about interaction with other systems.

The following example of a vision statement came from a workshop on organizational change in School District No. 45 (West Vancouver) in British Columbia. It is a vision for a learning organization. "Learning: anytime, anyplace, anywhere, anypace, anyone." Creating the practice, form, and function that enables this vision statement would be an exciting challenge.

PART TWO: THE SITE-SYSTEM RELATIONSHIP

The second part of developing the guidelines or touchstones for action resides in the creation of an information age site-system relationship. In the industrial age organization, sites tend to operate independently and are loosely connected to the center through accountability and performance measures as well as financial oversight. Sites have some commonality with the system, but they tend to evolve their own culture and their own independence. Traditionally there is not a high degree of cooperation or integration among or between other sites in the organization.

In the information age organization, however, both the site and the system work from the same common reference points, share common practice, and work as an entity to build, share, integrate, create, and apply knowledge to enhance the core purpose of the enterprise. Information about the organization should be available to everyone in the system so that they understand, support, and work toward achieving the overall goal and do so through knowledge about how the *pieces* contribute to that goal.

Site-based management models are common in industrial age organizations. Site-based models would also play a role in information age organizations but within a broader context than just management. How these information age models work and function is quite distinct and different from their industrial age cousins. Public education often uses the site-system management model in an attempt to flatten the hierarchy and involve more people throughout the organization in decision making. They want to avoid top-down decision making in favor of a bottom-up approach. There is an attempt to place decision making in the hands of those closest to the *action*. But not all sites are collaborative in nature and shared decision making is an anomaly.

The idea of shared decision making has merit, but often the implementation of the concept doesn't. In the existing site-based management model, each site is allowed to go in its own direction, creating priorities, innovations, practices, and procedures. There is little consideration of unity or coherence or systemic thinking. As well, when a crisis hits, the senior administrators often reclaim centralized powers and invoke top-down strategies with little consideration or involvement by the site. This usually creates significant organizational issues and tension within and among employee groups.

The information age site-based model for a public learning system would attempt to do many of the same things as its industrial age counterpart. It also uses the top-down bottom-up model but with one important distinction. The top-down model pertains only to organizational processes and the bottom-up model pertains to action or activity around those processes. The model "has to impart knowledge both as substance and as process—what the Germans differentiate as *Wissen* and *Können.*"[2]

The top-down approach in this context ensures consistency in expectations regarding learning, culture, equitable access to resources, purpose, and direction of the system. The bottom-up approach ensures that those who have the specialized knowledge and expertise take the lead. The core purpose of the organization is aligned with those expectations, and information, knowledge, and expertise within the site is shared across the organization.

Having the people closest to the problem provide input to the decision-making process is shared within both paradigms. But in the learning organization, decision making must be connected and integral to the whole system and not just one piece of it. Each site within this environment has a responsibility to address both systemic and site needs, to build and share knowledge, and to create collaborative structures that involve all staff in the organization in their areas of expertise. To do this requires some agreement as to the *what* of reform as a system, as well as some understanding of the *how* of reform as a site.

Site-based management initiatives within the existing culture of public education seldom generate any real change or reform because power and authority reside with the centralized authority. In other words, leaders talk about a site-based management system as a means of creating a more collaborative culture but limit or restrict who can decide *what* or *how* at the site.

Industrial age organizations thrive on centralized power. Even though the language to describe site-based management sounds like change, the models that are implemented do little more than support the *responsibility with no authority* reality. The challenge for the organization trying to implement fundamental change is to avoid replicating the past and creating a new relationship between the system and the site that is truly collaborative. But systemwide collaboration is not a hallmark of industrial age organizations.

Seldom is the implementation of this industrial model accompanied by overall expectations that promote system coherency and consistency. This arrangement has advantages when trying to meet local site needs, but it has little advantage in trying to meet system needs. System priorities include establishing common technology platforms and infrastructure, implementing meaningful curriculum, addressing the needs of special education students, and creating systemwide opportunities for professional development and training, such as establishing a common approach to the teaching of math.

Within this model, site leaders make decisions and choices without any requirement to collaborate and share information or knowledge with others. Often they make decisions based on their own beliefs and not on an analytical review of research or hard data on student achievement. There are no systems expectations for them to do so.

The industrial age model of site-based management works against the concept of the learning organization and the establishment of connections to other systems. It serves to sustain organizational environments that promote the status quo, past practices, and self-serving leadership, and compartmentalizes access to knowledge and expertise within the organization by focusing on one piece of the organization.

What is required is the creation of a new model that defines system and site-based responsibilities within the context of an information age organization and around what we know about learning systems. This definition needs to be closely tied to a governance structure that promotes and expects collaborative goal setting and assesses/evaluates performance outcomes based on both site and system performance.

This new model has the potential to be flexible, have a flatter organizational hierarchy, promote systemwide collaboration, and support situational leadership by staff, both formal and informal, depending on levels of expertise. Through knowledge building, sharing, and application, practitioners would ensure that the system enhances competency, that the research on learning is *always in play*, and that the needs of learners are foremost in everyone's mind.

Redefining the relationship between site and system requires the creation of a framework for decision making and the establishment of guidelines for organizational activity. This redefinition would include the following:

- Visions/plans are collectively and collaboratively set and support the organization's directions, goals, and expectations. They address the core function of the organization.
- Organizational success is defined in terms of how well the organization and/or individuals responded in terms of supporting, creating, or nurturing learning opportunities. Tasks set within this framework are measurable and attainable. These tasks must focus on educational renewal and connect to the system through an alignment of their role/impact on governance, leadership, instruction, assessment, evaluation, and technology.
- Environments are created that promote informed risk taking, involvement, communication, decision making, and collaboration. The organization empowers those with the most expertise to lead. Therefore, leadership responsibility will vary. These environments will redefine the relationship between organizational content and process. Most formal leadership is process driven. It creates the environment that will produce the results. Most informal leadership is content driven where those who have the knowledge produce the product.
- Leadership teams (also refer to chapter 13) have terms of reference that allow them to make decisions and choices within a framework of common expectations and guidelines set by the system so that there is alignment within the organization. Teams work at both the system and site levels and both have a responsibility to build and share knowledge—to a large degree. Teams are used to carry out the content activities of the organization.
- A process of objective measurement and evaluation around what the learner does, and not what the organization says the learner is doing, is established. The success of the learner organizationally and individually defines the success of the learning organization. This means that both the content and process of learning are assessed.
- Excellence in learning via skills and training, as well as knowledge acquisition and development, is a priority for all staff.

- The site-system model collectively establishes the *what* for the system and gives great latitude to teams at both the site and system levels to determine the *how*. Attention is also paid to the processes used at both the site and system levels by individuals and groups. In the information age paradigm, processes and content are equally as important. Both must be directly managed. In the industrial age model, processes are often addressed informally and sporadically.

NOTES

1. No reference available.
2. Peter F. Drucker, *Post-Capitalist Society* (New York: HarperCollins, 1993), 198.

Chapter Twelve

Understanding What Needs to Be Changed and Why (Generalization Two)

There is a danger of probing the future with too short a stick. Excellence takes time.[1]

Once the vision and the context for a new site-system relationship have been established and validated, the participants in the process will need to knowledge-map the organization.

Knowledge mapping helps ascertain what aspects of the organization fit within the industrial age paradigm and which ones fit or need to be developed to fit within the information age paradigm. This is a compare/contrast exercise that shows points of alignment with the vision.

The juxtaposition of these two paradigms serve as the starting place for discussion about what needs to change and why. Understanding the differences in the paradigms, as well as the specialized knowledge pertaining to each piece of the organization, is important in terms of valuing what is appropriate change and what isn't. It provides insight to the changes needed at the individual, organizational, and community levels.

It is also important to review and understand how the components or sites of the organization contribute and link to the systemic whole. It requires that the component pieces of each organization be reviewed with an eye to creating new practice, sustaining old practice, or eliminating the practice altogether.

The knowledge-mapping process creates understanding as to what should change, why, and what new relationship between the site and the system needs to be developed. The information and knowledge gained from this process will create the opportunity for organizational *transcendence*. The outcome should be that the pieces of the organization gain function from the vision, are structured around the new context for site-system relationships, and are interconnected through the knowledge-mapping process around common expectations about learning, practice, form, and function.

Each organization has its own individual character or makeup. For discussion purposes the following *pieces* have been selected as being representative of a typical public education organization:

• Governance
• Leadership
• Process and systems leaders
• Collaboration
• Process/practice of learning or its theory
• Financial management and business practices
• Learning communities
• Technology
• Values and ethics
• Assessment and evaluation
• Ethos for change

Each of the aforementioned pieces is outlined in terms of its Industrial form, function, and practice. The discussion also includes a consideration as to how each category might be changed so that it has an information age context. These perspectives are not intended to be definitive statements of what will or must be. Instead they are intended to *provoke* and *promote* a collaborative reflection and discussion about the nature and substance of change needed in each area.

GOVERNANCE

The governance model for overseeing public education has evolved during the past two hundred years. It was originally designed to provide parents with local representation and local control of their school system. The creation of school boards was a response to the need for system oversight and to ensure that the perceived learning needs of children were being met. In more recent years the role and purpose of school boards has been shaped and influenced by the bureaucratic requirements of the centralized systems to make public institutions accountable when and where the needs of the public are represented.

Educational governance, over time, has moved away from being a volunteer and locally directed activity. Trustees are paid for their service from taxpayer dollars and their responsibilities are closely coupled with regulations developed by government. At one point, the control of the system and financial decision making was in the hands of local communities. That control has slowly devolved to the centralized authority. Under the centralized authority, the role of the board and of trustees has become more political. It is not uncommon in the past two decades for individuals to run for trusteeship based on their support or rejection of the policies of the government. The primary focus of governance is no longer on system oversight on behalf of students and parents. It is politically motivated and many trustees align their interests, decision making, and the exercise of power to various personal or special interests.

This type of governance structure, built around personal or special interests, creates a dynamic tension between those dedicated to the profession of learning and those dedicated to political functioning and system control. The increased emphasis on politics and lobbying makes it more difficult to enact or implement substantive change or reform initiatives because politicians want to address the political needs of special interest groups. These special interest groups have no interest in participating in any processes around substantive change. Doing that might affect their power or control within the system and they want to ensure that this does not happen.

The balance of power between governance and senior management is out of sync more often than not. Job survival, whether rightly or wrongly, is causing senior managers to acquiesce to the political needs and wants of their boards. This acquiescence subjugates their leadership responsibilities and roles as advocates for students and learning to the political whims of nonprofessionals.

It is not uncommon for trustees, once elected, to directly involve themselves in the management of the system despite their lack of qualifications, knowledge, and experience to do so. Senior managers who allow trustees to influence educational decision making and management of the system do so out of fear of repercussions. This is wrong.

For some, trusteeship is primarily a stepping-stone to higher office or it provides a platform for the exercise of personal power. When this happens, the needs of learners will never take priority. It is the ultimate act of arrogance, and it does more than any other single issue to debilitate and create a dysfunctional organization. This is not to say that there aren't fine and dedicated people who served as trustees. There are. It is just that they are no longer in the majority and are not able to successfully impact on the political self-serving agendas of most boards.

The centralized control exercised by government and its bureaucracy, the process for allocating funding, and systemwide contract negotiations have contributed to the breakdown of governance systems. Politicians and bureaucrats at the center have implemented polices and laws that have expanded the influence and control of government as a means of ensuring systemwide compliance with policies or directives.

They make funds available to the special interest groups willing to cooperate and support the implementation of government agendas. These agendas often have little to do with local needs or priorities—needs and priorities that boards and their communities used to set.

Under these circumstances boards are mostly left with the responsibility for decisions made centrally but with little authority to respond to local issues or needs. The central systems manage the most artful of political maneuvers. They force local boards to make decisions that sustain government policy but keep government at arm's length from the implications of the decision. Local boards become a foil by which government can enact decisions but disavow responsibility for the outcome. The amazing thing is that the public, for the most part, remains blissfully ignorant of this reality. Trustee elections on their own tend not to draw a large turnout of voters.

It is time to think of another model of governance; one which embodies the concepts of the learning organization, reflects a wide variety of partnerships and community perspectives, and has the authority and mandate to act within preestablished parameters to empower communities and create local capacity to deal with change and local priorities.

Under this new governance model, boards would no longer be forced to comply with, or implement changes to, programs and services that were not part of the core program. They would have the capacity to make decisions based on knowledge or understanding of local issues, values, or needs. Government's role would be one of setting consistent standards and expectations for the whole system as well as ensuring that training, resources, planning processes, and accountability measures are in place. Government would determine what the core purpose and function of the system should be but local boards or councils would determine the processes for doing so.

The centralized government would still have control to ensure that legal expectations were observed, that resources were equitably shared, that a core educational program was offered in all schools, and that the needs of the society were being addressed. They would also ensure that schools were expected to meet required standards and expectations; standards and expectations that reflect the reality of the twenty-first century and not the nineteenth century.

What then would this new governance structure look like? Should it

- Have a broader mandate than just public education? Could it focus on the learning needs of a community and encompass other organizations like health departments, attorneys general offices, social service agencies, and postsecondary schools? It does not make sense to suggest that the governance system for learning encompass only kindergarten to grade twelve and represent only one organization given that learning in a knowledge-based society and economy is a priority for all members of the learning community.

• Focus primarily on developing community visions, support the change process, ensure appropriate resources are available to sustain community infrastructure in the service of learning, and assess and communicate progress or failure to the community on a regular basis?

• Require that the people who govern have some knowledge about learning and learning organizations? How can you govern what you don't understand or know? Learning and how people learn is too important to be left in the hands of well-meaning amateurs or politically motivated people who wish to use trusteeship as a stepping-stone in a political career or who wish to advance the cause of a special interest group.

The model for governance in a learning organization must, by its very definition, be substantively different from its industrial age counterpart. The focus on collaboratively setting expectations, measuring results, and designing policies, processes, and expectations around learning would lead to new structures and formats for governance.

Pioneering the Mindscape: Designing Learning Systems for the Information Age (1992) called for the "establishment of a Learning Council that would inventory community, resources, facilities and skilled personnel as well as the needs of all learners within the community. It would coordinate services and establish programs to meet the requirements of the community vision statement. A key role of the council would be to reconcile larger societal needs with the community's vision of itself."[2]

The idea of a Learning Council as a governance model has value and is worthy of consideration. There are many groups and agencies within our communities that have some responsibility for a component of the lifelong learning agenda. Our industrial age assumptions lead us to believe that there is some coherence among these organizations and the needs of communities they serve. This assumption is not accurate.

These organizations have no coherent strategy for working effectively together to serve the communities in which they exist. They are separate and distinct silos of influence. Their inability to collaborate and work together creates a system dysfunction around learning that is costly. Under these circumstances it is difficult to utilize all of the learning resources available to the community in a focused, reasoned, and harmonious manner. The concept of a Learning Council could begin to address these issues and could serve as the basis for creating a governance structure for a learning community.

Literacy, for example, is a topic that is being addressed by a variety of groups within communities: preschools, community groups, kindergarten to grade twelve classes, colleges, corporations, or people for whom English is a second language.

The value of literacy to citizenship, learning, and economics, and for reducing inappropriate behaviors, accessing postsecondary institutions, and improving access to the world of work is clear. Literacy is a *womb-to-tomb* issue and might be the place to begin uniting the community around a common need. It is the primary skill for accessing the industrial age society.

In the information age, this traditional definition of literacy is still important but so is technical literacy, numeracy, technology skills, process skills (e.g., critical thinking, problem solving), visual literacy, and knowledge about the fine arts and sciences, especially life sciences. These are the new basics. They are the tools that inform the new cognitive infrastructure needed to function successfully in a knowledge-based society. Therefore, it may be in the best interest of society, of communities, and of individuals to develop one governance model, like a Learning Council, that would provide a coherent and sustained approach to learning programs and services.

LEADERSHIP

"Every organization must be prepared to abandon everything it does to survive in the future."[3]

The relationship between governance and leadership is symbiotic. The effective functioning of one gives effective form and substance to the other. Leadership styles that honor the past, sustain the present, and/or ignore the future amount to personal and organizational malpractice and malfeasance. The right type of leadership guided by an appropriate governance model is absolutely critical. This point cannot be overstated.

It would appear that leadership in all areas is in flux, due to politics, self-interest, or the lack of systemic will to do anything that strays from the status quo. In fairness, there are leaders who are aware of what needs to change, but there is limited support for their thinking. No mandate presently exists within public education, or within the society it serves, to validate any leadership initiative that creates the type of change anticipated in this discussion.

Like Churchill, during the 1930s, as he watched and warned about Hitler, the leaders in the know are unable to do what needs to be done. They are frustrated and feel that they are unable to make any significant difference toward averting what some refer to as an impending societal disaster. Few leaders appear to be willing to go against the grain for fear of personal consequences.

They are cautious because the environment in which they work does not support informed risk taking. They will wait until there is community awareness around what needs to change and why.

Unfortunately, the type of reactive or anticipatory leadership that galvanizes a community, or an organization or institution, to action is sadly lacking. It appears that we have to wait for an economic, social, or political event to threaten the well-being of the community before there is movement in this regard. It would seem that it is part of our human nature to resist changing until the threat of great harm is upon us. It is usually when a doctor provides an unfavorable diagnosis that most people initiate some attempts to change their personal practices and behaviors. The same comparison holds true for individuals, organizations, and communities regarding their ability or will to deal with significant change. Only through inspired and informed leadership can there be attempts to avoid this type of outcome.

Wisdom suggests that we should initiate some change processes immediately based on present circumstances. We should not wait for an event or circumstance that threatens or brings harm to the economic, social, or political well-being of the community and its citizens. Our past history suggests that this type of wisdom is seldom applied.

Perhaps in the age of knowledge and with the creation of learning organizations, the type of thinking or wisdom we need might become a reality. The research on learning illuminates the pathways to change. The type of leadership we need to sustain learners and learning organizations is vastly different from what we are used to. Leadership styles that value lobbies, build personal power bases, and promote territorial imperatives at all costs are not needed. They are detrimental to the welfare and future of the community and the society.

Learning organizations need leaders who:

- will take informed risks;
- understand that the basic unit of change is the individual;
- understand the importance of individual and organizational learning to the change process;
- have fundamental understandings of the learning process; and
- have a sense of where we've been, where we are, and where we are going and why.

Our society needs people who understand systems and processes, as well as possess and demonstrate character, integrity, and values in their leadership processes. These leaders must have the ability to sustain parallel mindsets so that they are able to know what practice, procedure, innovation, or process fits within which paradigm and why. They need to be able to effectively communicate these understandings and to be able to take advantage of the manageable moment when they are able to shift, or cause to shift, from one paradigm to the other.

These leaders need to be able to see connections to other systems and how those connecting points can be built upon or strengthened. In public education, for example, there are needs for better links to early childhood education, to family literacy groups, to those responsible for improving parenting skills and supporting young parents, and to a host of other agencies and groups who are working and supporting families. This partnership is needed to enhance the readiness of children for the formal learning processes found in the public learning system. (See chapter 13 for more discussion on process and systems leaders.)

As well, there is a need for better links to postsecondary institutions and to the world of work. The challenge within the learning organization and within the community is to build a coherent set of processes and procedures that link organizations in a meaningful way so that they better meet the learning needs of individuals and groups.

If it is not a time for heroes, it is certainly a time for heroic deeds. We need to know, understand, and feel, at a very deep level, that the type of leadership needed to lead and manage an industrial age organization is not interchangeable with that needed to create a learning organization. We need to be aware that those who have much to lose by change and who have been rewarded and sustained by adherence to industrial age practice will not readily embrace new ideas and concepts that will abolish or substantively change what they have created or nurtured in their careers.

It is not known if the following anecdote is true or not, but it serves to demonstrate the danger of uninformed leadership.

General Custer was informed by his scouts about the size and nature of a force that was gathering in his area. He ignored the scouts and continued forward even though "the young Crow scouts thought death was certain, and when one named Goes Ahead began taking off his ragged Army uniform, and singing his death song, Custer asked through his interpreter what was going on. 'Tell him, that in a very short time, we're gonna be killed!' said the scout."[4]

Custer had the same information as the scout but he was *attitudinally and intellectually* unprepared to make proper use of it. Custer was well trained in the theory of military strategy and tactics at West Point and well trained in the application of warfare through his Civil War experiences. He was recognized for his competence and leadership skill, received many field promotions, and was recognized for his heroic actions. However, he was unable to adjust to the new realities that faced him because of his attitude and assumptions. His assumptions served to create a *fatal flaw* in his leadership processes, resulting in disaster for him and those he led.

He ignored critical information because of a mindset that prevented him from intellectually absorbing new data and adjusting his attitude so that he could use his skills, training, and experience to full advantage in an unknown situation. Clearly, leadership choices can be both good and bad. These are choices driven by value and belief. Leadership can provide opportunities to create and innovate as well as destroy or be destroyed. It can be enhanced by character or diminished by the lack of it. Being a leader can be something an individual creates or a group bestows.

We need leaders who know, on both a personal and organizational level, that they are attitudinally and intellectually prepared to lead in the conceptualization and functioning of a new public learning system. For others it will require a significant transformation and realignment of skill sets, attitudes, and mindsets before they should, or can, participate in the change process.

In an industrial age organization, most people are vulnerable to the whims of their leaders because the culture focuses on compliance to those in charge. It is a hierarchy of power. In return for their compliance leaders are given considerable latitude to exercise their organizational power around personal objectives and beliefs, sometimes to the detriment of the stated values and goals of the organization.

In the information age organization focused on learning, the emphasis of leadership has to be on practices and procedures that nurture learning and create knowledge and application. This perspective promotes leadership styles that focus on the needs of individuals, groups, and the system and limits the opportunity for exercising individual power. The needs of those whom the system serves take precedence over the needs of those who serve the system. It also creates a need for a system that allows people with different levels of expertise to lead, depending on what needs to be achieved.

When members of an organization meet informally away from work, or at a coffee break, they talk about leadership and the people who lead them. They tend to respond to leadership styles and processes in personal terms based on their perception of how they are treated or valued by that leader. Invariably, these assessments are quite different from the organizational or governance view as to what their leaders are doing and why.

The following questions reflect some of the ways employees in a learning organization might consider and judge leadership styles.

- Does the leader's style encourage me to go to work?
- Does the leader create a positive climate?
- Can we trust this person?
- Is this a person of good character?
- Do our leaders encourage us to be the best we can be?
- Do they set appropriate standards for themselves and those that they lead?

- Do they seek our opinion on the things we should be consulted about?
- Do they make decisions free from the influence of lobbyists and special interests and can they build a consensus for the decision?
- Does this person know where the organization is going and why?
- Can this person get us to work together in a positive way or does this leadership style keep us divided?
- Do they take, and allow others to take, informed risks?
- Can our leaders help people, both inside and outside the organization, adapt to change without creating chaos?
- Do they perpetuate self-serving myths about how well things are going within the organization?
- Are they able to help us set manageable and achievable goals that are relevant to the change agenda?
- Are they able to plan and promote coherence and consistency?
- Are they able to communicate, and promote communication, across the system?
- Do they stand for something that is good and do they have values and possess integrity?
- Do they have a sense of humor and do they like people?
- Do they know when to exercise power and authority in an appropriate manner?
- Do they believe the concept of learning organizations and are they able to create and sustain environments that enhance collaboration?
- Do they understand learning and how people learn, and are they able to apply those concepts to the design, processes, procedures, and structures of the organization?

Those whose style demonstrates these leadership and personal qualities are best equipped to serve the needs of a learning organization. These are leaders who can be trusted, share power, and focus on both process and content. They create environments by which individuals and groups can create, innovate, take informed risks, and excel.

People who exhibit these characteristics on a daily basis are exciting people to be around. The cultures of the organizations they lead promote participation, growth, and a desire to learn, change, and adapt.

Those leaders who put the learning needs of children first and foremost in their actions are admired by their staff and within their communities. Those who sacrifice the integrity of the system to curry the favor of politically motivated trustees or special interest groups or who lead as a means of serving their own needs are not.

There is no doubt that being a leader in public education is challenging. To properly lead in this environment requires confidence, knowledge, the ability to serve the core purpose of the organization, and a comfortable ego that can withstand personal attacks. Often leaders are hired into an environment in which special interest groups try to ensure that they won't try to change things too much. These groups also try to set processes in place that will limit what the organizational leader does and under what circumstances. Sometimes trustees are part of that process.

But not all leaders are there for the right reasons. The following tongue-in-cheek descriptors identify some of the negative leadership styles that are reflective of politicized organizations and systems, and are all too abundant within the industrial age organization.

- The Anointed Not Appointed Leader: He or she might make comments like "I have arrived; I am here to save you; I know the answers; I am complete and you will benefit from my knowledge and leadership."
- The Teflon Leader: These leaders design processes whereby others are accountable for everything that goes wrong and they are responsible for everything that goes right. They won't make critical decisions and will refuse responsibility for anything that they think could adversely affect their career path.
- The Articulate Incompetent: According to these folks, the universe is unfolding as it should, based on their perception of the politically correct position that guides their every action. The image they project and the reality of who they are can be worlds apart. They effectively use the language of change to describe actions and processes that are not what they seem.
- The Pater/Mater Syndrome: Leaders with this syndrome see the organization as a fortress or a last line of defense against unwanted and external intrusions by society. They enshrine the past. They take care of the custodial needs of the work group. Issues and problems are dealt with in a safe manner, past practice is deified, and meaningful change is nonexistent.
- The Bureaucratic, Anal-Retentive, Policy-Driven, Process-Mad Leader: These people follow the rules because they lack the experience or imagination to break them. Staffs are always in meetings, being consulted and pressured until they confirm the decision that was predestined by the leader in the first place. Policy or trends are used to justify actions that are in fact a product of their own personal leadership whims.
- The Single-Purpose Initiative: These individuals have been promoted to a leadership role because of excellence in a certain field of specialized knowledge. They operate or lead schools or districts from this narrow perspective, most often to the detriment of other programs or initiatives.
- The SOS Leadership Style: The motto for these leaders appears to be "we are under attack and taking on water." These leaders have a bunker mentality and

see threats in a variety of events or initiatives. The unions, the parent groups, the board, and the government agency responsible for education are perceived to be blockers of progress and provide excuses for inactivity. These people are constantly stressed. Nothing from their perspective appears to work and everything is phrased in the negative.

- The Egocentric Leader: This person usually confuses the difference between power and authority. Staffs are penalized, most often in a nonpublic fashion, for disagreeing with this person's profound view of the universe. The organization is managed and led according to how the events and activities of the organization impact personally on this individual.
- The Joker Is Wild: This leader is a gambler and takes uninformed risks. He or she has no organizational focus. There is a lot of activity but little progress.
- The Chameleon—You Can't See Me Style: "I will be whatever you want me to be," describes how this leader functions. The leaders are constantly jumping from one trend to another and never bring any task or activity to completion. They are known for trying to please those higher up in the hierarchy.
- The Placating Political Leader: These people function best by trying to keep every lobby group happy even at the expense of doing what is right for the organization. They will do almost anything to avoid taking a stand or position.

Leaders with these less than admirable characteristics promote organizational cultures that are:

- Negative. People do not have positive feelings about going to work.
- Low on risk taking or change because the price paid by members of the organization for not succeeding is too high. Mistakes are not tolerated because leaders perceive that a problem or mistake reflects on how they are viewed by their superiors in the system.
- Low on trust and with little belief in the organizational vision. There is a lack of organizational consistency and little innovation.
- Systemically dysfunctional and with little will to deal with problems or issues.
- Selfish and promote self-interest.

These leaders do not promote a culture that will embrace or initiate change. If an organization wishes to shift to being a learning organization then the definition of leadership needs to be stated in operative and measurable terms. People selected for leadership positions need to be chosen on their demonstrated ability to meet those expectations.

Governance must set these expectations for leadership and create the appropriate environments to support and nurture what they expect. They must also set the quidelines and procedures to recruit, train, or embrace leaders, at both the site and system levels, who will meet or exceed these expectations. These leaders should also be assessed on their ability to create, nurture, and support appropriate learning environments. There are many building blocks in the change process but governance and leadership are two of the most important ones. There can be no organizational trust if this relationship is not properly defined and understood, both philosophically and operationally.

NOTES

1. No reference available.

2. Everette Surgenor, *Pioneering the Mindscape: Designing Learning Systems for the Information Age* (Vancouver: EduServe, 1992), 25.

3. Peter F. Drucker, Management Quotes, www.managementquotes.blogspot.com/2007/04/every-organization-must-be-prepared-to.html.

4. Mark Bedor, "Preserving the Battle of the Little Bighorn: Joe Medicine Crow," *Big Sky Journal,* www.custer.visitmt.com/Joe.pdf.

Chapter Thirteen

Creating a Site-System Leadership Model (Generalization Two)

You see things and say, "Why?" But I dream things that never were; and I say "Why not?"[1]

The site-system relationship within the learning organization invites the creation of new leadership models. In the industrial age organization leadership is structured around the specialization of knowledge and very few people in the system have an overall or big picture view of the system. Leadership is in the hands of the few. Because the learning organization requires a formal balance between process and content, everyone within the organization needs to have a systems view if processes like knowledge integration and knowledge sharing are to have any effect. In this environment leadership will be shared by many.

These new leaders will need to be trained to work within a site-system context. The evolution of the site-system leadership model is based on a new relationship between the system and the site—a relationship that formalizes the leadership functions not only around the content of the organization but around the processes that drive decision making, collaboration, learning, and knowledge building. One person in the organization will have the overall system responsibility, but many people need to participate in its implementation. The development of this model is also guided by the second generalization about learning theory.

This type of leadership, needed to manage the envisioned site-system relationship, is not generally found in industrial age organizations. The creation of a position called director of homeland security in the United States after 9/11, albeit only a beginning, was an indication of the need for this new type of leadership in a new type of organization, specializing in both content and processes. The Department of Homeland Security is not being proposed as an example of what should be. In fact the opposite is true. The lack of success of

93

the homeland security initiative makes it quite obvious that the processes, practices, and organizational structures needed to support this type of leadership model have yet to evolve. That is because that organization is still led and structured around industrial age notions.

The site-system leadership model should be designed around the research on learning. Perhaps we might see the evolution of dual leadership roles in terms of content and process as we see in industrial age organizations between content and finance. Whether it is one or two people, someone will have overall responsibility for managing the processes of the organization. But in order for it to work, all participants in the organization must assume some responsibility to manage, and be informed about, both the content of the system as well as its processes.

The responsibility is to keep the content and process activities of the organization aligned with the organization's identified core purpose. In other words, there needs to be coherence and consistency between organizational processes and practices.

In the information age environment of rapid change, the organizational consistency and constancy is found in the processes, and the change or fluctuation takes place in the content. In the industrial age organization the opposite is true. General Electric, for example, would make and market the same toaster for twenty years. That would not be possible in today's environment where new is associated with better or improved.

The following is a list of the Process Leadership system and site responsibilities and duties in the learning organization.

- Promote a broad-based visioning process that is both consultative and collaborative. It would include the development of common reference points that support the *what* and *why* of the change initiative.
- Implement goals and directions from planning process.
- Create a positive environment around learning and knowledge to support change. This environment would address such things as trust, informed risk taking, integrity, and ethics.
- Evaluate progress of the organization against its stated outcomes regarding content and process.
- Ensure a systems approach so that there is a consistency of behavior and performance.
- Ensure systemic, not strategic, planning and accountability processes are in place.
- Communicate to the system on the activities, successes, and failures of teams. People need to know what does and doesn't work.
- Build partnerships with other appropriate systems or organizations that would expand the capacity of their system.

- Allocate resources according to need and ensure that everyone knows what the resources are, as well as how to access them.
- Ensure that the organization complies with societal/government expectations with regard to laws, rights, contracts, and implementation.
- Promote a systems view with staff and volunteers as a way of creating a culture that supports organizational adaptability and flexibility.
- Promote knowledge building and sharing throughout the system including the dissemination of information on new trends, practices, or initiatives.
- Promote excellence, quality learning, and knowledge building to ensure that the organization is always in a competent and relevant position in regard to its core purpose.
- Ensure that appropriate technology systems and applications are in place to support individual and organizational activity.
- Create cross-functional teams around expertise and interest, and develop support processes to assist individuals and groups to be effective.

These site-system leaders must be knowledgeable about learning, how people learn as well as how new learning impacts on the existing content and the processes of the organization. They must understand how learning processes help in the creation, implementation, and maintenance of organizational practices, procedures, and functions that address the organization's core purpose. They must know and understand the oral history, the culture, and traditions of the organization and must be able to reference or utilize these components in the change process. This must happen at both the system and the site level.

Process management must work in harmony with, and support the work of content management, or those who work in leadership teams. These content leaders and teams would:

- provide expertise in a given content area;
- structure teams and promote team activity that is within the organizational vision;
- have the ability to communicate, build consensus, and share with others the work and progress of the team;
- have the authority and responsibility for decision making within the team regarding the content of the work; and
- promote flexible attitudes and help develop team members to be able to learn and unlearn.

The relationship between the two leadership roles is reciprocal. Both have a responsibility to serve the core purpose of the organization to promote learning, knowledge building as well as organizational relevance and competence. The content leader must understand how his or her area of expertise interacts and supports the rest of the organization. The process leader must be able to see the connections between and among all of the components of the organization.

The goal of both categories of leaders is to create environments that allow those with the most ability, current expertise in an area, and talent to teach and learn, and to lead at the content levels at various moments in the life of the organization. To facilitate this requires new models for collaboration, information sharing and knowledge building, creation, and application.

In this context, the leader of the organization does not need to be the one who knows the most about the content. In the complex organization of the knowledge-based society, only some leaders will be masters of content. But all leaders must be masters of process and possess general understandings about organizational content. They need to do this to ensure that organizational expertise is organized and utilized to its fullest potential for the benefit and support of the core enterprise.

NOTE

1. George Bernard Shaw, *Back to Methuselah* (1921), part 1, act 1, Quotations Page.com, www.quotationspage.com/quote/26791.html.

Chapter Fourteen

A New Context for Collaboration, Leadership Teams, Learning, and Financial Management (Generalization Two)

Change and improvement are not the same thing. First we create our structures and then our structures create us.[1]

COLLABORATION

If content and process leadership are fundamental to the creation and implementation of the change process, then the creation of the collaborative workplace is fundamental to the quality and substance of the change. The notion of creating a collaborative workplace is not new. Industrial age–based organizations encouraged collaboration, especially in the 1980s and 1990s. Their collaborative model valued respect, interpersonal skills, communication, sharing of information, and problem solving as key components of the collaborative process.

At first glance it would appear that the industrial age collaborative model and the skills required to participate in that process could be transferred successfully to an information age organizational setting. A closer analysis suggests that this is an incorrect assumption. Although many, if not all, of the component pieces of collaboration model may apply, the context in which they exist in each paradigm is fundamentally different.

The industrial age culture and practice establishes a context for collaboration that is the antithesis of that espoused by the thinking contained in the learning organization and/or learning community. The industrial age culture can be characterized as follows:

• Unwilling to share power and authority through all levels of the organization.

- Believes that in most circumstances people can't be trusted to do the right thing and that workers can only be made effective and productive through leadership and management initiatives.
- Rewards and encourages personal loyalty to senior managers as opposed to rewarding and encouraging loyalty by all staff to organizational goals.
- Requires well-defined policies, expectations, and levels of accountability around production and defined discipline measures for those who step outside the expected norms for compliance within the bureaucracy.
- Sustains an assumption that the sum of the pieces automatically equals the whole and that fixing or changing the pieces will automatically be an improvement to the whole.
- Encourages or allows only a few people to see how the whole organization really functions.
- Places a primary emphasis on content or product.
- Promotes an attitude that the organization will provide products around what it believes, or perceives, society wants and needs.
- Accommodates changes but only within the context of a component or piece of the organization.
- Views organizational decision making and collaborative practices as top down or bottom up.
- Develops specific skills for specific tasks related to products or specialized areas of knowledge.
- Limits risk taking by employers and employees.
- Incorporates a political agenda that involves unskilled and uninformed individuals to participate in key decisions under a stakeholder or partnership tag.

The information age culture can be described as follows:

- People share power around expertise. The one with the most knowledge teaches others and co-leads the team with the person who has the responsibility for managing the processes or systems.
- Knowledge building and knowledge sharing is encouraged. All members of the organization are expected to acquire a systems view of the organization.
- Appropriate levels for risk taking are established with no disciplinary action for mistakes within those parameters.
- Management of processes and systems is formalized so that content and process are equally valued and the pieces are objectively and rationally related to the whole.
- Knowledge building and knowledge sharing are formalized across the system. This results in self-motivation and self-direction within the organization.

- People are encouraged to pursue their passions and interests, relevant to the organization's primary purpose.
- Structure is fixed around processes, and flexible or adaptable for content.
- The world is viewed in holistic terms. All of the pieces have a systemic connection.
- The organization is able to accommodate rapid and persistent change.

The comparison of the two cultures suggests why a significant organizational shift in how collaboration and collaborative efforts take place is needed, in order for the organization to have value within the construct of a learning environment.

The skill set required to collaborate in the learning organizational culture is of a higher level and is more complex than its industrial age counterpart. It is structured around the notion of personal and organizational competence. This collaborative process requires participants to utilize a systems view to ensure the alignment and coherence of procedures, practices, and processes within the organizational structure. This process promotes knowledge building and knowledge sharing within the site and across the system. This type of collaborative process would have to be expanded upon, developed into a rational set of skills, and taught to members of the organization. It requires new practice.

In order to be sustained within the organization, these concepts of collaboration need to be embedded within the governance and leadership models and strongly connected to learning processes. In public schools this connection would apply to the learning and instructional models by which practitioners manage both the content and process of what is being learned. Instructors would need to be able to demonstrate and utilize practices based on the research on learning and have learners be able to demonstrate what they have learned through real-world applications.

LEADERSHIP TEAMS

The idea of leadership teams is not new but the idea of leadership teams using an information age model of collaboration is. These teams provide those with the most knowledge or expertise within a specific area the opportunity to apply that knowledge or expertise to the attainment of both the systemic goals of the organization as well as their own area of specialization.

Both process and content leaders, as a means of engaging and involving individuals, utilize these leadership teams at every level of the organization so that the organization is able to maximize the human potential of all of its members.

The use of these leadership teams within the organization will

- Create a practice that assesses the reality of the organization and compares it to the ideal or desired reality (i.e., what could or should be based on the trends and realities of the new paradigm). This requires team members to constantly identify, validate, or reject individual, group, and organizational assumptions, perceptions, and presumptions as a beginning point for collaboration.
- Enable the development or creation of the collaborative descriptors to be used in the creation, implementation, and application of change processes and functions within the organization.
- Constantly align organizational activity with organizational goals and expectations. Doing so creates organizational coherence. Points of dissonance or places where no coherence exists become opportunities to make changes to the process or to recommend changes to the process or system manager.
- Honor the building and sharing of knowledge as a means of creating and sustaining individual and organizational relevance and keeping the focus on learning.
- Encourage questioning, challenges, and appropriate risk taking by all members of the organization.
- Share individual, group, and organizational expertise, information, and/or knowledge in an open way so that all members of the organization can acquire the knowledge and build upon it.
- Encourage people to challenge their thinking processes whenever something has been achieved or completed so that they start thinking about the next level. By anticipating and preparing for the next reality or the new challenge, individual and organizations can avoid complacency and satisfaction with the status quo.

As with any good learning experience, prior knowledge is considered a base upon which these teams can build, access, or integrate, share, or develop additional knowledge. It is also the reference point for the participants to *unlearn* in order to acquire new knowledge as well as to use reflection and scaffolding of information to build knowledge in terms of content, product development, decision making and leadership.

The task of preparing team members to utilize these processes is a leadership responsibility. The team leader's responsibilities would be to

- listen to team discussions;
- alert the team as to when they are making decisions from an emotional, not objective, base;

- challenge the assumptions/perceptions the team used to support its discussions; and
- ensure that the team is looking at current knowledge, trends, and information.

The team leader would facilitate the research of issues for the team, ensure that timelines and reporting structures set by the team are acted upon, and involve the team in looking at the issues under discussion from as many perspectives as possible.

Having these skill sets formally identified and assessed as a leadership responsibility, whether it be at the system or site level, or at the process or content side of the organization, would be a significant change from current practice in promoting the development of the collaborative workplace.

Leadership teams used in this manner provide an opportunity to flatten the hierarchy of the system and to create a more inclusive environment for decision making at both the site level and across the system.

The team leader would also be responsible for

- inviting participation for a team;
- selecting the team in terms of experience, expertise, and partnerships;
- having the team confirm performance criteria by which they will measure their success;
- managing the resources attached to the goal in a fair and equitable manner;
- convening meetings; and
- ensuring that
  - minutes are published;
  - the information regarding the team's activities is communicated throughout the system;
  - a report is filed with the board in relation to achievements;
  - team members have information, research, access to opinions, and responses, in a timely manner; and
  - team activities are aligned with the overall goal of the organization and that knowledge building and knowledge sharing with all members of the organization is a primary task of the team.

LEARNING

Learning is a vulnerable act. As children we were conditioned to relate our ability to learn to acceptance, rejection, right or wrong, good or bad.

If we learn well, are raised in supportive environments where risk taking, the love of learning, and intellectual pursuits are prized, we are more likely prepared to continue to learn, to make mistakes, to ask critical questions, to value insightful and creative thinking, to make predictions, and to grow in an open and public way. We are also better prepared to reflect upon the assumptions and perceptions that guided our decision making and learning processes.

If, however, we come to believe that we are not as capable as others to think and learn, we are more likely to spend a lifetime rationalizing, adjusting, and trying to accommodate new learning within a negative emotional environment supported by inadequacy and self-doubt. We are likely to reflect and learn silently out of fear that our thoughts and ideas might be adjudicated as *less than*. If so, we will tend to make decisions and to hold on to beliefs that are based more on emotion than fact because we lack the skill, ability, or desire to validate our beliefs through interactions with other learners. Good learning experiences promote confidence and a willingness to extend our capabilities.

In the end, the way we approach our opportunities to learn has more to do with character and ego than it does with intelligence and creativity.

How then does one create a learning organization if it is peopled by learners who feel less than, where mistakes are viewed as incompetence or a lack of ability, and where who you are as a learner is judged by what you know or don't know as opposed to how you learn or could learn.

It would seem that we have some way to go with understanding the importance of learning not only to the practice of instruction, but also to leadership, collaboration, change, citizenship, and organizational form and function. Many leading proponents of educational change speak about learning as if it were a given that our education systems are skilled and knowledgeable in that area. The assumption is that education systems are about learning and that their practices constitute the basis of a learning organization. The research in *How People Learn*[2] clearly demonstrates that this assumption is incorrect and needs to be challenged.

We need to develop a new practice that addresses the individual needs of the learner and moves the system away from the industrial age practices of teaching to the average or to the group. It means changing the organizational focus away from information dispensing, to learning. The requirements for changing the current system include creating:

- New instructional practices—practices that are not commonplace within the classrooms of North America. The complexity of developing instructional practice to match what is presently known about learning is substantially more complex and at a higher level than the existing instructional skill set provided to teachers by teacher training institutions. It also exceeds what is generally considered current classroom practice.

- New assessment models that provide data for learners regarding what has been learned and what needs to be learned. This is quite different from gathering data on groups of learners for political reasons of accountability. This assessment model would provide the learner with a correlation to other outcomes and career aspirations relevant to the acquisition of specific outcomes. For example, in grade eight, math learners would be able to see why it is important to learn a concept because it is the building block for another concept in grade ten, which is also required to qualify for a postsecondary aeronautics program. This type of assessment provides learners with a complete, up-to-date transcript of courses and learning outcomes when they want or need it and in a manner that promotes relevancy and meaning for what is being learned.

- New uses or applications of technology that will allow system integration of software so that data on student learning can be collected from a variety of software or web-based sources in the system.

Learning outside of the classroom has become extremely important. If the aim of the organization is knowledge building and sharing of knowledge as a way of creating meaning and supporting application of what has been learned, then it stands to reason that learning theory will impact on leadership styles and will influence the way we communicate, share information, partner with other systems, collaborate, build teams, use technology, and plan. The learning environment must expand beyond the classroom.

Learning is also integral to the way we view and apply values and ethics within the organization. In short, what we know about learning provides insight to the creation of substantial reform for every aspect of the public learning system or learning organization.

We know that there are social, emotional, and intellectual aspects to learning. A positive learning environment will create a sense of community among learners that honors and values learning. If the learning environment is not positive, the opposite is true. Either environment can impact on how the system is organized, structured, and made operational.

Learning, both from an individual and organizational perspective, becomes the primary focus for the public learning system. This is also true for any organization that wishes to fully participate and thrive in an information age culture that values knowledge. Designing the content or primary purpose of the organization around learning, as well as the processes to manage, lead, plan, create, collaborate, and make decisions provides the demarcation point between the two paradigms.

What we know about learning provides insight as to how to approach the individual and organizational assumptions, presumptions, and perspectives that block or support learning. It helps us understand what must be unlearned in order for new learning to take place, both within the system and within the community.

It also suggests criteria around which we should develop governance models and leadership strategies, as well as to the selection of leaders. It informs us about the need to create environments that support learners and learning and suggests organizational issues around power distribution, collaboration, communication, content and process management, partnerships, site-system responsibilities, accountability, and resource allocation.

There are also implications as to how we use learning with technology and, more important, how we shouldn't use technology. The research on learning applied to the current way technology is used to promote, create, or assist learning opportunities suggests the need for many changes.

FINANCIAL MANAGEMENT AND BUSINESS PRACTICES

Learning organizations need to have processes that demonstrate systemically how their business processes are linked to the core activity of their enterprise. They need to do this in order to utilize their resources in the most effective and efficient manner possible.

Business functions are not normally included as part of the educational change process. Educators complain that the economics of education are never understood by the business administration. Those on the business side argue that they need to control the expenditures of educators. They do not see educational ideas or practices as being firmly rooted in the real world. Generally, both sides see their parts of the organization as distinct and not closely related in terms or purpose, function, and accountability.

In the learning organization, all of the pieces of the organization must be formally connected. Those areas responsible for business and financial management must be part of the data gathering, the assessment, and the planning for the entire system. It is the only way for the organization to develop, resource, and sustain organizational changes.

The business practices of the organization must be current and efficient. They must be connected to the process of developing the resources and capacity to implement the changes defined by the planning process. Financial management and accountability as defined by Alfred Sloan[3] at GM in the 1950s, can't continue to be the model for auditing and assessing how well the system is doing.

Industrial organizations address reform of financial and business practices through a process called *reengineering*. People who promote these types of processes suggest that you can modify the existing financial structure as a means of facilitating change. The process has value for the learning organization, as well, but only when it is placed within the context of information age thinking. Some benefits gained by evaluating and assessing the financial and business practices of a learning organization are that they:

• Provide an organization with the opportunity to understand the purpose of its business processes and to determine if they are connected, aligned, and add real value to the overall goal of the organization.
• Allow an organization to increase both the efficiency and the effectiveness of its business processes by streamlining the flow of information, the coherence and consistency of practice, as well as by the adoption of best business practices.
• Allow for the business and financial processes to be well documented, which provides all stakeholders with information that is generally in the hands of a few people in the organization.
• Enable the organization to strongly connect its business practices to the core activity of the enterprise (i.e., learning).

With a process like this, an organization could find that it is sustaining a practice or activity that is very time-consuming but not really necessary. It may also find that it is serving the needs of special interests at the expense of the rest of the organization.

A small district in rural British Columbia was able to initiate a business process reengineering, designed around information age concepts. Educational Data Systems (EDS) Canada partnered with the district and was responsible for the facilitation of the process. The process included a review of financial and business practices. The district faced serious enrollment declines. They also wanted to ensure that the learning services to students were the best that they could offer. They recognized that in order to be successful in the delivery of learning services, they would need to be more effective and efficient in the way they conducted their business processes.

They saw the review as a way of identifying necessary resources that could be reallocated to support new reform. The intent of the study was not to reduce staff. Instead, the belief was that any efficiency gains identified through the study would translate into more time for practitioners to spend on the business and services of learning.

All of the key people involved in the change initiative were first involved in a collaborative process to explore and understand the need and nature for systemic organizational change. Throughout the study, the group focused on three major questions developed by the district as part of the process to examine key components of the system:

- What practices/functions do we sustain and/or improve?
- What practices/functions are not present but needed?
- What practices/functions do we stop doing?

The study was structured around five stages: Project Planning, Current State Assessment, Conceptual Redesign, Cost/Benefit Analysis, and Recommended Next Steps. Project Planning began with an overview of the process and how it would be conducted. This was presented to all participants. As well, the processes were linked to district initiatives and thinking about change.

In the Current State Assessment component, an analysis of each process was undertaken to assess how well it functioned (e.g., what works well, what doesn't work well, what could work better). District staff provided the analysis and assessment.

The Conceptual Redesign component of the study asked participants to consider opportunities for the future and established whether these opportunities should be classified as Quick Wins, Short-term, or Long-term Opportunities. In the Cost/Benefit Analysis stage, the measurements for time on task in the current and the conceptual redesign were compared in order to determine efficiency gains. Finally, a plan was presented for how to most effectively achieve the identified opportunities as well as the training and resources needed to implement the changes.

The key finding from this study was that with the implementation of the redesigned processes, the district achieved a 15 percent efficiency gain in the current cost of its administrative and bureaucratic processes. It was anticipated that this efficiency gain would translate into a win for learning in the district.

This process created an opportunity for substantial change within the district because it was incorporated as a part of a systems reform, was connected to the overall purpose of the organization (learning), and prepared people for the process by having some exploration of the assumptions, perceptions, and presumptions that guided the existing system.

Five years later this change process continues to evolve with varying degrees of success. What has become clear is that the process of connecting a review of financial and business processes with the core purpose of the system has sparked a number of key initiatives as well as changed the mindsets of participants. The system did not move forward as far or as fast as originally anticipated, but it was able to become proactive and positively affect the downward trends it was dealing with.

The reengineering process presents the possibility of generating 10 to 15% savings across the system that could be applied to change and reform initiatives. The process could fund things like a revitalized curriculum, a new instructional and assessment model, a longer day, a longer year, higher wages, and the acquisitions of communication and applied technologies. No new money would be required and the process could be self-sustaining, as long as bureaucrats didn't siphon the savings off to serve other projects and activities.

NOTES

1. No reference available.
2. National Academy of Sciences, Summary, *How People Learn: Bridging Research and Practice,* M. Suzanne Donovan, John D. Bransford, and James W. Pellegrino, eds. (Washington, D.C.: National Academy Press, 1999), www.nap.edu/html/howpeople2/notice.html.
3. Alfred Sloan, as quoted on Mario Vellandi's "Melodies in Marketing" blog, January 28, 2008, www.vellandi.wordpress.com/2008/01/28/alfred-sloan-and-organizational-management/.

Chapter Fifteen

Community (Generalization Two)

People have one thing in common. They are all different.[1]

The terms *community* and *neighborhood* are interchangeable. Whether the communities of today, or the sometimes idyllic remembrances of past communities, have the capacity, wisdom, insight, and knowledge to deal with the changes we now face is a question that should be under active discussion. If your frame of reference is the industrial age, then your answer to the question would probably be "yes." If it is anchored in the information age, then you most likely would say "no."

There is certain nostalgia about the past, especially in light of today's societal upheavals and lack of predictability. Some community members wish for a return to a time and way of life that had more normalcy and consistency. But mindsets that enshrine the past serve only to block organizational and community change. Instead of looking forward, people pine for a time gone by. It is the same thinking or feeling that initiated a back-to-the-basics movement in education.

This nostalgia for community resides mostly with the boomers and seniors. Many boomers grew up during the 1940s and 1950s. Community life at that time was still influenced by an agrarian culture, the development of suburbs, the growth of factories, and an abundance of natural resources. It was a time where one could still find mature forests, untouched streams and rivers, a vast array of wildlife, and a commitment to family values.

In many locations the community hall or community center was the centerpiece of the community—the place for family and community celebrations. Education in multigrade settings was not uncommon. The majority of citizens valued education and saw it as a way of getting ahead in the world. There was an expectation that youngsters should go to school to learn and conduct themselves according to certain community values.

The message at the supper table from many parents was about going to school and getting an education. Parents wanted their children to do better than they did. Education was viewed as a gift and was clearly attached to a child's hopes for a productive future.

But there was also a corollary belief that if you tried to learn and couldn't, then school wasn't for you. The world of work in those days still offered many opportunities. After all, people concluded, not everyone was smart and capable of so-called book learning.

As well, children grew up knowing that they were expected to conform to certain community values, especially those values that pertained to respecting people's property, the authority of adults, and the importance of money and property. This was not always the case but it was more common than not.

Communication and information about society came primarily via the radio, the emerging medium of television, and the weekly newspapers. It was viewed as a wonderful environment in which to grow up. But are the perceptions about that time and that way of life correct? It needs to be examined because it is a view of community that keeps us looking backward instead of to the future. It is a view that will impede the change process.

It is clear now that some of the children who grew up in that period of time suffered in silence from sexual abuse at the hands of their family and others. It became apparent that many adults knew about these abuses within the community and looked the other way. In that period of time, what took place in the family generally took precedence over what took place within the community. Ignoring things like incest and sexual abuse was part of the culture.

The youth of the 1950s and 1960s modeled what they saw among the adults of their community or neighborhood. Drinking and driving were culturally acceptable. Teenage pregnancies were not uncommon and were responded to with quick marriages or long leaves of absences from the community.

The schools of that period are not always remembered with great fondness. Some teachers were physically mean and demeaning. Many kids never made it past grade eight or grade nine. They were made to feel that they were not smart enough to compete. It is a feeling that many of them never forgot. They had to leave school and enter the *real* world of work. This distinction between learning and work reflects an attitude that still haunts the structure and format of secondary schools today. It is a distinction without validity in the information age. To be successful today you must be both a learner and a worker.

Another area for comparison of past to present has to do with violence in schools. This insight might be questioned but the schools of the 1950s and 1960s were far more violent, on a day-to-day basis, than they are today. The use of firearms and weapons today by kids against kids adds a new dimension to this, but these incidents are not daily nor are they systemwide.

In the 1950s there were numerous fights among kids and sometimes between teachers and kids during school hours. People saw it as a reflection of a way of life in which you stood up for yourself and responded to an understood and shared code about right and wrong. People were independent and did not have a lot of need for government or expectation for government services. They took care of the things that needed to be taken care of.

Compare those experiences with the communities of today. No matter where we live we expect a wide variety of community services to be available, and we expect those services to be equal to what everyone else receives whether they live in rural or urban areas. We have high expectations for infrastructure (roads, water, sewer information, and increasingly, telecommunications) and services, especially services that ensure our health and safety. In the past, alcohol abuse significantly affected some communities, but today alcohol, drugs, crime, as well as all types of abuse and health issues significantly impact most communities.

The only thing that seems to unite or speak to community today is the coming together to deal with a tragedy or disaster. We unite more around what is wrong than we do around what is right. As well, the *I/me* syndrome also helps to separate us. Some people never see or speak to their neighbor. They don't want to or need to. From this perspective, the communities of our past had a greater sense of identity, purpose, and togetherness.

There are many aspects of those past communities or neighborhoods that are still valued today. But it was not a superior way of life. If it were, how can we rationalize what the generations of our parents and ourselves have done to forests, streams, oceans, fish stocks, wildlife, and water fowl? The comparison of our present realities with those of our past is not a straightforward task.

We are further impacted in our concept of community life by unlimited access to the media and the Internet. Communication is instantaneous and global. Most news focuses on the negatives of life in the global community, creating in us a sense of a society gone to hell. This can't help but impact on our perceptions of our communities and our society.

Because we live in a global information system and because it's primarily the negatives that get reported, we know much more about life in the global community than probably we have a need for. The composite picture of tragedy, heartache, and political dysfunction presented many times a day is bound to make people cynical, distrusting, and threatened.

When news was primarily local and regional, there was a different focus. The news tended to be more positive, respectful of privacy, and not always intended to define that which is worst about humankind. Those reporting the news today would say that they are only reporting what we, the public, tell them we want to see. The old expression about getting the government we deserve could be rephrased to say that we get the media we deserve.

These comparisons of community bring a realization that neither the communities of our past nor those of our present would be able to support and nurture the learning organization needed for the twenty-first century. It is not about the past being better than the present. It is about defining what was best about both and using those as design or reference points for the learning community of the future.

Most community life is no longer about a group of people living in an area with a majority view about common values and beliefs. The more common determiner of where you live seems to be dependent on economics, diversity, technology, and lifestyle. We need to accept and value diversity, independence, and creativity, but we also need to establish some reference points about the *common good*. The problem is that without some notion about how to work together for this common good, the creation of the learning community and the creation of the public learning system become extremely difficult.

Perhaps the journey of discovery that leads to the re-creation of community and to the development of learning organizations begins with a better understanding of *why we are*, *what we are*, and about shaping *what we might be*. The community of the past was not all that we believed it to be. Going back to that time will not create the culture necessary to sustain the learning community. Nor do the communities of the present have that capacity to do what needs to be done.

The promise of the information age culture is about having what you want, when you need it, in the form that best suits your needs. Learning communities, however, are something different. Not only must they address individual needs but they must also serve the needs of communities and organizations or systems within the community. The information age culture requires us to work in new ways: ways that support systems working with systems.

Perhaps the starting point for community renewal is to look at the only thing that is common to, and necessary for, all aspects of community well-being—learning. At present, the community of the past and the community of the present lack the capacity and understanding to create information age organizations. Learning is the only common theme that binds us together.

Serving individual needs is one thing, but there is also a need to service group needs. The rights of the individual need to be closely coupled with responsibility, but there must also be some recognition regarding the rights of the group within the context of community life. It is a balance in need of definition.

Community life must be about the higher ideals contained in the philosophical notions of a civilized society. Citizens must be self-disciplined and obligated to unstated beliefs and principles around the common good about behavior, ethics, and values. This speaks to the self-discipline and responsibility of the individual acting within the framework of a community code of accepted practice and procedure.

An Internet search provides a number of examples around North America and Europe of communities that are trying to develop mechanisms and/or processes for rebuilding. They have created partnerships that allow them to capitalize on the collective wisdom expertise and resources of community in order to enhance their quality of life.

Certainly the idea of building knowledge and sharing information within and among our communities is not new. In the 1700s, Ben Franklin and others attempted to systemize the identification of dissemination of knowledge and information.

"It was characteristic of Franklin to combine theory and application. But he found knowledge for knowledge's sake to be an unsatisfying formula. The kind of knowledge he prized was that which made life easier, more productive or happier."[2]

Franklin developed a strategy about identifying and sharing new knowledge in the American colonies. He proposed the formation of the American Philosophical Society. Members representing a broad range of specialization would discuss new innovations or research within their specialty areas, and the society would attempt to disseminate the information among colonists. Although this proposal met with limited success, it did constitute an early effort at creating a learning community.

But our realities are quite different. The initial starting place today would be to invite community agencies, organizations, and service providers to come together to consider these strategies:

- Developing an organizational framework that would allow all agencies to work cooperatively toward common goals.
- Enhancing the capacity of our communities for dealing with cultural, social, and/or economic issues that threaten our quality of life and the standard of living.
- Confirming a value system that identifies the standard of behavior and expectations that we believe enhances the quality of life in a community.
- Understanding the assumptions, perceptions, and presumptions we hold about organizations, leadership, learning, and so on, and going through a process that validates and confirms these beliefs within the context of what we know about the emerging postindustrial culture.
- Creating an environment in which knowledge and opportunities are shared for the benefit of all.

We know that communities across North America are faced with many difficult challenges that threaten the way its members live, work, and organize. Economic factors have resulted in a loss of jobs and the reduction in services such as social, health, law enforcement, and education. These reductions, in turn, have impacted on the quality of community life. These communities struggle to understand the workings of a global economy.

The World Trade Center attack in 2001 and the implementation of the legislation around terror have brought changes to privacy rules and impacted on personal freedoms. These new practices around surveillance and privacy signal significant changes to what used to be. They are not yet fully understood. Add to this the HIV/AIDS and SARS epidemics, and the Asian flu pandemic, stem cell research, and cloning. The complexity of citizenship has substantially changed. The challenge to keep informed and to know and understand what is true is sometimes overwhelming.

But not all of the threats to a better way of life are external. Within our communities, some citizens are supplying and/or creating the demand for drugs, shoplifting, vandalizing, stealing from work, making false insurance claims, misusing sick days from work, stealing cable and satellite service, overfishing, polluting, and littering. It is not one individual or group. It is widespread. Some people rationalize their behavior by saying that if big business and/or government cheat, then it is okay for them to do so as well. It would appear that the motivation for many community members to undertake the self-discipline and obligation of citizenship around the common good is in jeopardy. The obligation for creating better communities requires changes at every level and within every sector.

The key and fundamental aspect of achieving all of this is a *can do* mindset within the community, an ability to be proactive about change, and an understanding that the issues and concepts that hold true for individuals regarding learning, also apply to organizations, institutions, and communities. It is possible, for example, for a community, as well as individuals, to learn new things and unlearn old ones.

The difficulty in building a learning community should not be understated. It requires knowledge, insight, expanded definitions of literacy courage, and new mindsets and skill sets to accomplish the task. Corporations in the industrial age culture talk about retooling and reengineering as a means of staying current and relevant. The same concept must be applied to creating a knowledge-based cognitive infrastructure within ourselves that helps us to manage and make decisions, as citizens, workers, and individuals within a society.

The knowledge base we must deal with (e.g., technology, security, safety, travel, health, government, information, and communication) is significant.

Without this knowledge we are subject to the whims of those who have it. Knowledge is power, and if power is not equally shared, then it will be used to the detriment of some and to the benefit of others. This is exemplified in the comments of a television newscaster who said that his job was to interpret the news for the listeners. This is a dangerous notion. The future of our democratic society is based on having an informed citizenship—citizens who are qualified to make their own judgments and decisions, both as individuals and as members of strong communities. As citizens we need to be on guard against some corporations, organizations, institutions, politicians, and special interest groups. We need to have the knowledge and judgment to know when they are shaping messages. These messages are usually wrapped in the greater good. They sound factual and appeal to values and beliefs, but they are really intended to cover an action designed to advance public or corporate policy for personal or special interest gain.

NOTES

1. Robert Zend, quoted at UBR, Inc., www.people.ubr.com/authors/by-first-name/r/robert-zend/robert-zend-quotes.aspx.
2. H. W. Brands, *The First American: The Life and Times of Benjamin Franklin* (New York: Anchor Books, 2000), 168.

Chapter Sixteen

Technology (Generalization Two)·

We are more about common gadgets in our society than we are about common sense.[1]

Billions of dollars are spent annually across North America on the delivery of kindergarten to grade twelve programs and services. Public education systems perceive these dollars to be *untouchable*. They act as if this money will always be there. And no matter how much money is supplied for education there are those who will constantly argue that it is not enough. These professionals continue to believe that they are in control of the future of education and learning as well as the pace, nature, and substance of any change within that organization. They are wrong on all counts.

Their naiveté is found in the way that many educators respond to the emergence of private schools, expanded home learner programs, and the development of traditional schools. They see them as small intrusions into their monopolistic enterprise. The alternative delivery responders and the business community, however, are under no such illusion about the state of the industrial age school system or about the dollars that fund it.

They want access to these dollars. They have been experimenting with online instruction models, software, curriculum, as well as assessment and data management tools over the last fifteen years in an effort to create a competitive model to public education. Most have only digitally emulated the existing structure of school in an online format, but some others are starting to see something quite different.

When this different concept about school and education emerges, it will offer a suite of programs and services around an *anytime, anywhere* delivery. It will customize service around individual and/or group needs, and it will employ multimedia tools, quality software, and learning resources, broadband access, and most important, effective e-learning models of instruction based on learning and how people learn. Technology will be the primary environment by which these programs and services will be delivered.

This model, when it is developed, will have a significant impact on the traditional structure of public education. Technology and technology tools coupled with an understanding about learning and its importance to the knowledge-based society and economy will provide the impetus for this change. Once this model emerges, consumers will be able to make choices about education based on their needs, lifestyles, their perception of values and ethics, and their desire for their children to be equipped to be successful in the global society. Technology is certainly an impetus for the deregulation of the public school system, but is that the right outcome?

The arrival of the new model will have its greatest impact at the secondary level. It will break apart the notions of time and control that have been a dominant characteristic of the secondary timetable and, indeed, public education. It will allow learners to hold jobs and to engage in learning at times that are convenient for them. But social interaction in the teen years is still a powerful force and may be a motivator for sustaining some aspects of the existing structure. This remains to be seen. It may be that peer interaction, participation in athletics, fine arts, or lifestyle programs might be handled by community centers instead of schools as part of community learning programs, involving both secondary students and adults. The Learning Council certainly envisages this type of community-based learning model.

Will this model appeal to everyone? Probably not. But what is the impact if schools lose 20 to 30 percent of their traditional clientele? Under existing financial formulas a loss in student population of 20 to 30 percent might have a disproportionate impact on programs and services. That, coupled with the 5 to 15 percent who have already selected models other than public education, makes this issue quite significant. Will these events precipitate the collapse of the public education system? Who will get hurt by this and will public education be allowed to evolve into a multitiered system where access to the best services is dependent on wealth and location?

The current model of technologically delivered educational programs and services only exacerbates this issue because it continues to be an extension of what is. Continuing to sustain the Industrial school system by using technology to replace existing school-based delivery models will only widen the gap between the *haves* and the *have nots*. In this circumstance, technology is being used as a substitute for teacher-led programs and services. It is primarily a financial, and not a learner-driven, solution. Technology is not the villain but its usage by industrial age thinkers and planners is. Replacing classrooms and teacher-mediated services with an online mentoring service, as it is presently structured, is not in the best interest of most learners. The success rate of students using these services is woefully low.

It is not an issue about the technology, but it is an issue about old practice being delivered in an even more ineffective model than the existing classroom. Technology linked to processes that build on learning, engaging curriculum, new assessment models, and quality instructional approaches with opportunities for reflection, peer interaction, and values discussions has value as long as the issues of equity and access are addressed within the society.

But the advent of this model is not something that government, communities, and most particularly, schools are prepared for. Under present circumstances we lack the collective wisdom and leadership within the bureaucracy, within governance, and within communities to ensure that this model develops the right way and under conditions that best serve societies and the common good.

If technology is one of the major creators of change, then we need to understand its influence, its potential, its weaknesses, and its utilizations and applications, specifically as they apply to learning and more generally as they apply to the society in which we live. It is not something we should fear. Technology might change the work, but it will not lessen the importance of a teacher, especially one who is skilled around learning. "Any teacher who can be replaced by technology should be."[2]

Technology is a tool, an environment, and a way of thinking. It can be perverse, exclusive, embracing, restrictive, enabling, and enslaving, depending on who is using it and for what purpose. Technology is reshaping our world. Its influence is felt far beyond the classroom. By looking at that extended application we can understand some of the answers to the questions about its application to learning. The following examples highlight how technology is reshaping our world.

1. The outsourcing of jobs to the developing world is a source of concern within North American society. There seems to be little recognition or concern that the first wave of outsourcing took place within North America itself. We have chosen to pump our own gas, pay more for banking services while receiving less return on our money, use automated tellers (and sometimes even pay for the privilege), and arrange our own travel and purchase items online.

Corporate America understood who we as citizens had become. It knew that it could use technology to eliminate jobs and reduce costs and that consumers would accept less service and even, in some cases, pay more money in return for being able to customize or personalize choices around ease of use, time, and location. The *I/me* agenda caused us to have less choice as a group, less service, and higher costs in return for individual preference.

2. Back in the 1980s and 1990s, two groups understood the connection between networks and the need for rapid global communications. They were the American military and banks. The American military established a global network as part of its strategy for defense of the United States and the banks established a global financial system. At times these financial systems seem to be able to supersede the power and control of individual nations, their goals and values, as well as the *common good* of their citizens. Financial systems are making choices about the world economy and the production and cost of goods that seem to be beyond our government's ability to control or regulate.

In effect, technology has been used to provide a small group of people huge control over the daily affairs of individuals in the global society. What the banks did has become a model for other commercial enterprises like oil companies. When systems like these become monopolies, service and choice are replaced by profit and self-interest.

3. Many of the classic television shows of our time came from the 1950s, 1960s, and early 1970s: an era of free television signals, lots of competition, and high quality.

The 1990s saw the creation of multimedia conglomerates. They control the movies, newspapers, magazines, news and regular programs on television, Internet services, and music. As a consequence, we pay substantial annual fees for entertainment that individually was less expensive. All television programming was free at one time. Some would argue that the product we now receive is less entertaining, repetitive, and overly advertised.

Technology in this case has been used to control the market, increase profit, as well as reduce quality and choice of programming. This is an example of thinking, behavior, and business practices reflective of the industrial age paradigm and its view of systems. News programs are now thought of as entertainment. In some cases critics say that the news reflects the message or messaging that the special interests who control the media want us to hear.

4. The impact of conglomerate thinking also applies to software and the Internet. At one time the Internet was free of spam, pop-ups, and viruses. Now various providers are trying to control access to the Internet and set the conditions and costs for use. The promise of a tool or resource that enabled a free society is being threatened and limited by these conglomerates.

If some of these companies have their way, we will pay for every e-mail we send. Bill Gates has proposed the equivalent of an electronic stamp that Microsoft would control. As well, we are forced to use proprietary software and specific gateways to access the Internet and are stuck with the limitations of those applications. The technology is being controlled and managed to yield maximum profit for the longest product lifecycle these conglomerates can inflict upon those who use their products.

The software we need to work, manage, and learn within knowledge-based organizations does not yet exist. Or if it does it is not being put on the market. We need software tools and applications that support the concept of learning, knowledge acquisition, application, and integration. Without them it will be difficult to utilize the processes we need to develop new practice, form, and function.

When conglomerates get involved, competition and service are reduced. The consumer is stuck with what these providers will offer. It is not necessarily about what he or she wants or needs. Telephone companies continue to block rural community access to broadband services and applications like VOIP because the business model doesn't support their implementation.

The economic, social, and political future of rural communities is dependent upon affordable access to true broadband. Despite that reality the monopolistic industrial-thinking phone companies won't provide the service, but neither will they allow competitors or local groups to do it on their own. This is just one more example of a mindset that puts these companies out of touch with the people they are supposed to serve. The problem is further exacerbated by the fact that many of the citizens in these communities have no understanding of why broadband services are important.

5. There are many examples of specialized technology available for personal entertainment and socialization, such as IPods, DVD players, cell phones, and computers. People, especially the young, are enamored of the latest gadget, its speed, capacity, quality, and price. In this area the competition is extreme, and consequently the prices and choices favor the consumer.

These toys or tools provide people with considerable options pertaining to personalizing their world. Certainly this technology changes practices as it pertains to communication, global connectedness, speed of messaging, and options regarding entertainment, sometimes for the common good and sometimes not. At times these services enhance the I/me syndrome at the expense of community and engage people in ways and for periods of time that may not be physically or mentally healthy.

But these types of technology are sometimes used to invade people's private and personal world, to illegally download music, movies, and satellite signals, and to create digital communities of common interest around special interests like games, art, clubs, bands, bomb-making, racism, hate, and pedophilia. Is this use of technology evolutionary or anarchistic?

It is also clear that given the choice, not all people are governed by the traditional ethics and values that guide the common good. Self-interest and self-indulgence, two key themes of the I/me society, seem to hold sway. We need to understand that as we build networks around the globe and create global interoperability, we are moving from an environment of multisystems to that of a few systems. It is like a global lymphatic system that sustains life, but once an infection is introduced, it can threaten the well-being of everything that is connected.

6. There is a concern about the power of messaging encased in digital imagery as well as the impact that software design has on patterns of thought and decision making. We often will reflect upon what we read but seldom question what we see. Digital products allow people to shape visual images as part of their messaging process, and we have not yet developed the skill set to question the digital images that are presented as well as how they are presented. Shaped and repetitive images are presented by mainstream media and on specialized sites on the Internet. They are not always guided by fairness or truth, nor are they always accurate. They are being used to emphasize a personal or special interest view.

DigEuLit is a group whose goal is to develop a European framework for digital literacy. Their goal is to formalize thinking around digital literacy so that it becomes part of their educational practice. We should be doing the same in North America.

7. Businesses are using technology to lengthen people's working day and to monitor work habits and productivity. This practice impacts on an employee's quality of personal and working life. Technology used in this way is an abuse and is reflective of an organizational and leadership style that has little trust or faith in people. It creates workplaces marked by suspicion and distrust. It is an industrial age application. Technology's promise in the learning organization—of greater freedom, creativity, more independence, and greater flexibility in the workplace—is not always fulfilled in this environment.

8. New vehicles are a pleasure to drive. The technology within these vehicles is complex and beyond most people's ability to repair when it fails to work. It is designed to be *time limited* to ensure that there is a whole secondary industry built around repair.

Why should the repair process be so costly—be so *exclusive* in terms of knowledge, and why do components need to be replaced as often as they do? Again this feels like conglomerate thinking that uses technology to control the market, as well as the innovations and the quality control of the product. It is not about excellence and it does not place the consumer first.

The technology used in these vehicles is so specialized and sophisticated that few people have the knowledge and skill to effect repairs. Does it have to be this way? In the industrial age era, a large segment of society had a general knowledge about how things worked and how they could be fixed. Is this knowledge domain so exclusive that the same can't be done within the context of the information age? It seems that when the knowledge is in the hands of a few, the consumer pays more. This is the antithesis of the organizing idea for the information age.

Of course, the discussion about technology is not all one-sided. There are many places where the technology is being used in fascinating and in good ways, like medicine, some genetic research, investigations of natural phenomenon on earth and in space, global mapping, and systemwide messaging like Amber Alert.

Technology, its infrastructure, its applications, and its accessibility are significant to our future. They could help with the provision of better educational and health services, involve more people in the political process, and assist us in solving our problems around energy, reliable food products, disease-free living, and poverty. At present its application and use within the society, apart from personal use, is industrial age. If it continues to remain in the hands of industrial age thinkers who are interested in control and profit, then it will be difficult to realize a common benefit for all humankind.

This conglomerate or monopolistic thinking and its impact on products, services, and quality does not only pertain to banks, media companies, and automobile manufacturers. It also applies to pharmaceutical companies, gas and oil companies, the food supply, technology, air travel, and large retailers. An argument could also be made for the inclusion of centralized governments in this group, based on its present use of technology in the delivery of educational, social, and health services.

This brings us back full circle to the role of technology in a learning community. Technology has the capacity to sustain the past, ensure the present, or create the future. This understanding requires us to review the research about learning and then ask how the technology best serves those functions. We then need to ask if the introduction of information and communication technologies into the classroom has fundamentally impacted on instructional practice in the classroom.

In most cases we would find that these technologies have been used to improve past practice, have created some efficiency but have seldom been used to support, create, build, and sustain the practice and procedures needed to create learning environments and opportunities based upon how people learn.

As long as we continue to take satisfaction from the fact that our education system is good, and in some cases excellent, at industrial age tasks, we will fail to see that we are losing our capacity to compete with those who wish to offer programs and services to learners outside the realm of public education. In our existing society, public education continues to fulfill the role of an information provider and not that of a knowledge builder. Educators seem to be unable to adapt to the reality that the niche for public learning systems in the learning communities of the twenty-first century rests in providing customized just-in-time learning services to learners in a high touch/high tech environment.

Peter Drucker, in his book *Post-Capitalist Society*, identifies how technology will change the way we learn and teach. He also speaks to the importance of the new technologies of learning and teaching to our culture, as well as national and economic success.

Drucker makes the point that the West underwent an earlier technological revolution in the seventeenth century around the printed word and that this revolution allowed the West to assume a leadership role in the world. He also says that China and Islam failed to adapt or adopt this technological revolution and fell behind. This decline served as the source of rebellion in both China and Islam.[3]

One only has to look at the number of public dollars at stake to understand why the competition for educational services will become fierce. A noncompetitive, nonchanging, and monopolistic public education system will not have a hope in being part of what is changing—it will only be part of what has changed.

It is important to ensure that public education systems participate in and become part of change processes. It is a challenge that must be met. The old adage about "doctor heal thyself" is apropos. We need qualified teachers to lead the learning process—teachers who have new skills, mindsets, and insights, and who use new pedagogical models, applied curriculum, and new assessment models. Technology as it presently exists is not able to replace a teacher skilled in the practices and processes about learning and how people learn. The fact that some people see technology as being able to replace what is currently being offered in a number of classrooms should be an indication of what needs to change.

In the era of printed textbooks that are out of date shortly after they have been printed, we need to develop high quality and engaging core curriculum that is delivered via the technological medium in a consistent manner in every classroom. This would allow for constant revision and update and would ensure a common standard and expectation for what is being taught and assessed in every educational circumstance.

How to use our technology in a way that helps communities, citizenship, economics, learning, health, and political engagement is a challenge. The technological advances we have seen to date are somewhat overwhelming and generally beyond the ken of most citizens. People are in awe of *what is* or *what might be* in terms of technological innovation. Their understanding of technology does not go beyond personal devices used for personal communication or entertainment. They do not yet understand what it is they should be fearful of or guard against with respect to technology. Nor do they conceive how the society we live in and the democratic values we cherish are threatened by these technologies.

The combination of information knowledge and technology allows a small percentage of people who truly understand the trends and realities of this new paradigm and the technologies it employs, to dominate the majority, whether it be through economic, political, or social means. As a citizenry we are woefully uninformed about so many things.

In the knowledge-based society and economy, citizens need to have new skill sets, understanding, and mental models to work from, including the uses and applications of technology. The price for participation as a citizen in an information age democratic society is much higher than it was for previous generations. Citizens need to have the knowledge or the processes to acquire and/or evaluate knowledge in order to provide a *check and balance* to the influence or desires of special interest groups.

Part of that check and balance might be the evolution of bloggers. Time will tell. They had a significant impact on Howard Dean's run for the presidency of the United States in 2004 and continue to play a significant role in the primaries leading up to the presidential elections in 2008. They were also instrumental in Dan Rather's removal as anchor for the CBS news.

It will take time to see if the structure of blogging, including video or v-blogs, will become a tool for citizens to voice their opinion to elect representatives and to demand changes to something in the society they find offensive. Or will it become a tool of specialized interests, be they corporate, institutional, or fringe group. Although blogging has had a significant positive impact, it was also used to attack candidates in the 2004 presidential election in a very biased and targeted manner.

That government agencies are trying to find ways to regulate bloggers and blogs should concern everyone. It affects governments' ability to control the message, and therefore is a threat to special interest groups. Traditionally small, well-organized groups within society have been able to have an impact on social, economic, and political decisions that impact on the whole society, often without its input or consultation. Blogging holds forth the promise of giving some organization and control back to society as a whole. It also has the potential to be a medium for hate and gossip.

The World Wide Web supports the development of an interactive global system for communication and information. Any global ill that invades the Internet could impact on any connected community. The unimpeded rush to put information on the Internet has provided individuals with opportunities to invade, sometimes in a significant manner, the privacy and security of an individual. As these systems grow, they have the potential to impede on our individual and collective ability to communicate, do business, or access accurate information. We need to learn as a society to ask critical questions so that we can ascertain what is true or what is being misinterpreted. Asking the right questions is the beginning of all quality learning experiences.

The Internet has proven to be of immense value, but it also allows some people who have no support in their community to form electronic communities of likeminded people for the purpose of evil intent, such as the Nazi movement, as well as spreading hate and child pornography. They work against that which the majority in our society value. The technology gives them a power and a voice that they would never find in most communities.

These are some cautions and concerns about technology, but without it the changes we need cannot take place. The Internet brings access to critical information and research tools to the doorstep, allows improved opportunities for economic access to global markets, can enhance communication within community, can become a tool for learning as well as the creation of learning opportunities, and can be a fundamental building block in the creation of a public learning system.

Technology, including the use of web tools, access, and applications will also help integrate the content and process functions of the organization; build, share, and integrate knowledge; share information across the system; enhance opportunities for collaboration; and support systemic decision making.

NOTES

1. Conversation with C. Surgenor, Fall 2007.
2. Arthur C. Clarke, 1993, homepage.mac.com/dcarroll2/2002/TESL2/lecture11.htm.
3. Peter F. Drucker, *Post-Capitalist Society* (New York: HarperCollins, 1993), 195.

Chapter Seventeen

Values and Ethics: Sustaining the Culture of Change (Generalization Two)

A people that values its privileges above its principles soon loses both.[1]

Values and ethics although not formally a component of most organizations, play a large role in how the information age change processes will be conducted and sustained. The traditional values that are perceived to have sustained earlier communities are currently challenged by practice, by other beliefs, and by individuals who choose to put their needs and wants above those of family and/or the community at large. The increasing challenge to organizational policies and procedures by individuals and their lawyers speaks to the trend of the individual versus group needs, and of the prominence of the *I/me before we* syndrome.

Community values and ethics are complex. They cannot be easily mandated or enforced. Values and ethics should be attached to reason and to perceptions of equity. There is a strong belief that the concept of equity has been severely challenged through the efforts of the government and social engineers who give preference on the basis of age, gender, culture, size of population, or special interest. The problem is that many of our citizens expect our politicians to exercise judgment on behalf of all citizens in an equitable way and on behalf of the common good. That is a fundamental concept of democracy. But it is not the nature of the beast unless there is some oversight and that oversight is dependent on an informed and involved citizenry who share a perception about right, wrong, and the common good.

Rightly or wrongly, many people in communities believe that the idea of *one law for all* no longer exists. This is a critical issue because it is highly unlikely that communities can create one belief about the common good unless there is a parallel belief about equity that is social, economic, and legal in its context. This is a values and ethics question.

The issue about a loss of values and ethics in society is reflected in the fragmentation of our communities. We are constantly faced with the question of whose values and whose ethics are they and under what conditions are they employed. We do not seem to have any common agreement as to what is right or wrong. This ambiguity is reflected in the decisions and practices of our courts, schools, health systems, policing systems, and community organizations. The concept of criminal and civil justice has evolved over the past two hundred years. It is now challenged by an emerging concept called social justice, whereby an individual's social circumstances determine his or her rights and responsibilities. The concept of social justice gives rise to differing perceptions about equity and fairness. Our society struggles with ways to resolve these issues: issues that tend to speak about how we are different rather than how we are alike. These differences are creating, not resolving, social conflict within our communities.

The focus on learning and how we learn limits the differentiation among us and puts all citizens on an equal footing with equity of access and opportunity to the society in which we live. Consider the following: "Somebody offered a $25,000 reward for information on kidnapping a child and at the same time there was a reward of nearly twice that amount to find the killer of a dog."[2]

The equity and opportunity issue is exacerbated by a lack of compassion or empathy for the less than favorable circumstances faced by some of our citizens. It would seem that many people in our communities have become indifferent to other people's suffering. They believe that individuals are responsible for their own condition and should therefore suffer the consequences for whatever that condition brings.

People are criticized for being homeless, poor, uneducated, and unemployed. The perspective is that these people are to blame for their own condition, and if they really wanted to they could do something to change their condition. Pope John Paul I often spoke about the culture of life whereby those who have, help those who don't. Warren Buffet, who at one point ranked as the second richest man in the world, is donating billions of dollars to the Bill Gates Foundation because of this issue. And Bill Gates recently announced his retirement from Microsoft to devote his time and energies to charitable work. Certainly many citizens devote countless hours to volunteer to help others, but there are enough people who don't care, which should be a concern to all of us.

The comments about values and ethics are not a call for the implementation of the doctrines of organized religions or for a consideration of the various interpretations of morality. Instilling religious views of values and ethics into the structure of the learning organization would only serve to further divide us. This is not a criticism of religion but recognition that religions don't have a common or united view on the topic. Picking one set of religious values and ethics over another would quickly cause significant community upheaval. Learning and how we learn is to a large degree neutral and somewhat free of bias. But a good learning environment has an inherent values and ethics component. The change process offers an opportunity to consider the development of values and ethics around learning as it relates to governance, leadership, and expectations for the system. The handling and sharing of information as well as how we work with others and demonstrate respect for diversity of ideas and opinions could also be included in that consideration.

Communities that begin to place a higher value on learning and the acquisition of knowledge can initiate these considerations. Institutions providing learning services must do so in an engaging way but there will be little opportunity for success unless learners make a personal commitment to excellence and performance. Having faith in the future and seeing a connection between learning and personal and societal success is a prerequisite to creating a value pertaining to self and community. Lifelong learning is a requirement and not a suggestion. Many students are dropping out of school, at rates of 10 to 13 percent a year in North America. A lot of work needs to be done, and quickly, to restore the value and purpose of learning and education.

The communities of the present and future will also have to deal with increased electronic visual imagery around violence and inappropriate values. A 2007 television ad showed a boy trying to hit a softball through the window of the house. When he finally succeeds, his mom comes to the window and gives him a thumbs up for his actions. The inferred message is that mom and son, working together in a devious and unethical way, have conspired to create a situation in which dad must now give her the windows she deserves.

This ad is disturbing for a number of reasons. Technology has been used to create an image that on the surface appears to be a play on boys being boys. On a deeper level, this image is about subtly manipulating people and activities to produce a selfish and self-serving outcome. It is trying to create an acceptance for a product through means that should defy community norms. This television mom is without values or ethics and this ad works against community.

The issue of violence and displays of inappropriate values on television, in the movies, in music, and in software games is also a growing concern across North America. Is it a matter of a corrupt society developing an appetite for that which defines the worst about the human condition? Or is it a matter of the majority of people in our communities not having the processes and structures by which to control, at least on a personal level, those things which they find most offensive? The solution does not rest in the elimination or prevention of these activities but in providing individuals and groups with the skills, knowledge, and insight to select what they want and eliminate what they don't.

There will be no appetite in the business community for product elimination because there is a growing market demand for products that are violent, sexual, and contrary to community norms. Sales indicate that these products are desired and supported by a significant number of people in our communities. What is missing is the discussion regarding the contextualization of these issues within a family/community environment; a contextualization based on empathy and around some basic precepts of right and wrong.

In short, the appropriate remediation of these issues rests within our capacity as human beings in family or learning units to unite around some common ideals and beliefs called values and ethics. These ideals and beliefs could be transferred to our practice as consumers, and a united practice could lead to a substantive change.

Appropriate values and ethics support a quality of life within the framework of community and support and nurture the concepts of the learning community. If we fully understood the impact of electronically created images on what we learn and how we learn, we would exercise more care about what access our children had to such opportunities. We would also actively work to provide them with frameworks and mental models from which to make decisions. This reinforces the concept that needs to become part of a new definition for literacy: interpreting and understanding the impact of visual imagery as it relates to messaging.

The need for this ability to interpret is reinforced daily in the media. At a time when it is projected that nearly one of every ten people in the United States will need food stamps to survive by the end of 2008.[3] When jobs are being lost in record numbers, when home ownership is declining, when energy costs are rising, when healthcare is a problem, and the dollar is being devalued, how does one listen to an ad about the promise of the future and not be cynical? Politicians and leaders of corporations are sending messages about citizenship, opportunity, taking care of the environment, and solving the energy crises that defy reality. They are trying to create images around what should be and present them as what is. One has to question the values and ethics behind this type of visual engineering.

Values and ethics are emotionally laden topics. These proposals about establishing community norms, especially those for a learning community, around the intrinsic values and ethics of a positive learning situation are both optimistic and hopeful. It will take much discussion and reflection to see if there is some way of formalizing these concepts within the fabric of the learning community. But how can you create organizations around learning and knowledge building if you don't include values and ethics to sustain good practice?

NOTES

1. Dwight D. Eisenhower, Inaugural Address (January 20, 1953), Quotations Page, www.quotationspage.com/quote/2027.html.

2. Timothy Egan, "Loyal Two-Legged Lobbyists Raise Banner of Dog Rights," *New York Times*, March 25, 2001, query.nytimes.com/gst/fullpage.html?res= 9A01E6DB133CF936A15750C0A9679C8B63.

3. Erik Eckholm, "As Jobs Vanish and Prices Rise, Food Stamp Use Nears Record," *New York Times*, March 31, 2008, www.nytimes.com/2008/03/31/us/31food stamps.html?_r=1&oref=login.

Chapter Eighteen

Assessment and Evaluation (Generalization Two)

Say what you have to say, not what you ought. Any truth is better than make-believe.[1]

In a learning system there must be the ability to monitor, assess, evaluate, and change or adjust whatever has been implemented and to do so in a valid, open, and timely manner. It is continuous and is the way that an initiative stays relevant and current. In an industrial age culture assessment and evaluation are also important, but they are periodic and somewhat external to the process.

In order to be effective with a knowledge-based planning model the models for assessing and evaluating both the content and the process need to be embedded in the change process. It is the basis for continuous improvement.

This requires assessment and evaluation models to be reconceived and developed around the three generalizations of learning. These processes inform both the individual and the organization as to:

- organizational and systemic consistency and coherence regarding both process and content (or the lack of it);
- the performance or organization in relation to its overall purpose and goals; and
- areas for renewal, *unlearning*, knowledge building, and knowledge sharing.

The assessment and evaluation process systemically links all of the components together. It can be designed to provide feedback on one or more systems at the same time and around the same outcomes. It also provides the information and feedback around which to design, develop, and implement the next phase of the planning process.

Assessment and evaluation processes are a major component of existing industrial age accountability processes within public education. They include authentic assessment, portfolios, performance standards, and district and school accreditation models. Some of these initiatives have value, but only when they are reconstructed within the context of the information age.

This form of evaluation and assessment process places a significant focus on results-based planning and performance standards. Unfortunately, the assumption upon which they are based is that the practices and standards we use as reference points for success are appropriate for the information age paradigm. Organizationally, this is a fatal error in that these practices and standards are reference points that keep us reflecting our past instead of anticipating our future.

Most states and provinces in North America keep *trend data* over a period of time to assess and compare student progress. What is the significance or value of comparing performance data around industrial age competencies and practices? How does that inform the public regarding the skills, attitudes, and attributes needed to function in an information age paradigm?

The primary purpose of assessment and evaluation in the industrial age organization, whether it is for assessment, content performance, or identification of special learning needs, is for the purpose of satisfying the centralized bureaucracies and their accountability agenda. It is done to serve a political, not a learning, need.

We have become so infatuated with assessment and evaluation that we no longer ask if what we are assessing or evaluating is still relevant. We are consumed with creating a perfect past. This process is intended to respond to what the public believes is important, and there is no attempt to try and create awareness around what learners need.

A prime example of this is the current refocus on literacy. We are using a literature-based definition of literacy. This type of literacy is important because it is our primary method of transferring our culture from one generation to another. This form of literacy is also key to how we access information.

This definition of literacy was, and still is, extremely important. It is one of the critical skills needed to participate in the industrial age information-dispensing organization called public education. But it is not enough. Literature-based literacy skills are not readily transferable to areas requiring technical, digital, or financial literacy.

In the information age, public learning system literacy (both literature based and technical reading and writing), numeracy, sciences (especially life sciences), math, digital and technical literacy, critical thinking, and problem solving are the critical basic skills to participate in a learning system. Most definitions of literacy include a reference to the world of work. But saying it doesn't make it happen.

We must adjust our curriculum and instructional strategies to include these skills so that we can provide learners with the ability to be literate in the information age workplace. That is not the current reality. We continue, with some exceptions, to sustain only the literature-based definition of literacy in our curriculum offerings, instructional strategies, and assessment processes.

This leads us to continue assessing and reporting on where we have been and not where we should be. Measuring past practice only serves to sustain the status quo. It prevents renewal. This perspective must shift to be built around the organizing idea for the future, around the content and process of learning, and around the needs of the individual or group, and the organization.

The collection of data around prior learning in an information age culture helps learners plan for and regulate their learning. An assessment profile designed around prior learning and applied learning would provide both the student and the teacher with information as to which concepts have or have not been learned and how the mastery of these concepts provides building blocks, or inhibits further learning. In a knowledge-based society built around individual and group learning needs, individuals and groups would use this type of information to help build lesson plans for learning. Not only does it support the relevance for what is learned but it also provides data to help guide the learning process.

It would be valuable, for example, to be able to furnish individual learners with comprehensive learning profiles over a number of years that show the attainment and level of complexity of learning outcomes they have mastered, as well as ones they didn't learn. This information about prior learning could assist learners, teachers, and parents in developing meaningful learning plans in regard to what they need to learn, how what they learn is connected to other learning, how well they applied what they learned, how it connects to what will be learned, and what relevance that has.

This is hard to do, if not impossible, under present circumstances. Software programs are often single purpose and proprietary and do not allow an integration of all of the data that is available in various locations on an individual's progress or achievement level. And the assessments by the centralized bureaucracies do not provide this kind of information. Current assessment practices are a response to a political need for quality control.

To change this process requires a change in thinking, a new culture designed around the organizing idea for the information age, new practice, as well as the development and implementation of software programs for data gathering and system integration at the classroom and school levels.

Instructors would be able to use this type of assessment/evaluation data to plan activities, sometimes collaboratively with the learner, that lead to understanding and transfer for the purpose of knowledge building, meaning, and application. It allows the instructor to incorporate, where appropriate, activities around collaboration, teamwork and practices, values and ethics, and use of technology. The assessment and evaluation data gathered would speak to skills, attitudes, and attributes gained, specific objectives mastered, and performance levels attained. It would also provide the means for students and teachers to plan, direct, and regulate individual or group learning.

As well, it is critical to the success of the learning organization that there are processes of organizational assessment and evaluation to ensure that the system is doing what it said it would do according to the planning process. Similar processes need to be developed around learning and leadership to help define and implement changes that would support change in these areas within the organization. Accountability levels derived from this type of assessment and evaluation would be far more meaningful than those that are currently in place.

Not only does the assessment and evaluation process assess and evaluate learner performance, but it also serves to do the same regarding the organization with respect to its central purpose or function. Specifically, it could assess and evaluate how the *pieces* (i.e., governance, leadership, process management, partnerships, technology, and values and ethics) are aligned and functioning.

It could be the responsibility of the Learning Councils to use evaluation and assessment data gathered from this process as well as feedback forms from students, parents, and community members as a means of accrediting their schools' and the community and/or parents' roles in making it a success or a failure. Some of this could be done online using weekly sampling procedures to assess performance as do some airlines and hotels seeking systemwide feedback.

Now that would be accountability. A lot of protections would have to be built into the process to prevent inappropriate practice or comment, but it could be done. And if it works for schools, it could work for colleges, healthcare providers, and possibly police forces. It has a democratizing notion about it that places responsibility upon citizens at the local level to participate. In doing so it promotes involvement in local, not centralized, processes.

NOTE

1. Henry David Thoreau, www.psymon.com/walden/quotes.html.

Chapter Nineteen

A Paradigm Shift in Planning— Implementing the Knowledge-Based Planning Model (Generalization Three)

A vision without a task is but a dream. A task without a vision is a drudgery. A task with a vision is the hope of the world.[1]

Systemic or knowledge-based planning is designed around the third generalization of learning. It applies to individuals and to organizations as well as to process and content. The organization's ability to plan, direct, and regulate individual and group learning and its ability to use the information about learning to create the organizational form, function, and practice to support learning is essential.

Strategic planning has been one of the cornerstones of the industrial paradigm. It embraces the thinking that produced the Maginot Line, the inadequate defense of Pearl Harbor, and produced the Edsel. It may be strategic and somewhat systemic, but it does not embrace systems thinking within the context of the information age.

The strategic planning process brings people together to plan a future and to make needed changes or adaptations for the organization. People participate in the planning process based on their knowledge of the present and past history of the organizational *piece* for which they have responsibility or for the special interest group they represent.

The assumption that drives this planning process is that building around the needs and directions of the *pieces* will create a coherent and consistent *whole*. The use of the word "strategic" conjures up images of a military intervention: an intervention that is decisive, powerful, and advantageous to the victor. Many people believe that strategic plans are a means for the organization to unite around a common direction, and an opportunity to implement reform and create meaningful change.

Nothing could be further from the truth. Not one of these prior educational planning endeavors in my experience ever brought substantive change, and seldom, if ever, did the plan ever unite the organization around the common good or its core purpose. Strategic planning serves a paradigm designed around the pieces, and the pieces always take precedence over the whole in this process.

Most people participating in strategic planning exercises come to the process with a desire to protect against anything that might provide a threat to the piece or component of the organization they represent. Logistically it is difficult to achieve the objectives of a strategic plan because only a small percentage of employees and partner groups participate in the process. Therefore, only a small portion of the organization has any commitment or belief in what has been developed. The plan is not known to all, and therefore, all can't anticipate, or reflect, the needs and realities of the whole organization. This type of planning ignores the process needs of the organization and makes minor accommodations, if any at all, to existing practice.

For the knowledge-based planning model to work, the people involved in the process must be prepared to participate. Knowledge building takes time and must be continuous. To create a new organization for a new paradigm, planners will need to have a clear understanding of the industrial age and information age paradigms. They need to know how the paradigms are similar and how they are different. They will also need some knowledge about the key elements or components of the system for when they are developing a plan, how these elements or components work, or don't work together, in the system, and how the creation of organizational coherence allows those in the system to better focus on the core business of the enterprise.

They also need to understand how learning takes place. They need to know all of this before they even start the planning process. This is no place for the uninformed or the well intended. Participants as well as planners need to be qualified to participate. It is not something that people of good will, but with no knowledge, can sit down and accomplish in two days. It is not accomplished through executive summaries. The knowledge building and deep understandings needed to redesign organizations so that they will function effectively and efficiently in the new paradigm take time to acquire. Therefore, the planning process must be systemic and not strategic.

The planning process must be strongly connected to the primary purpose of the organization, as well as to its processes, values, and partnerships. Planning also has to consider how technology might be integrated into these activities and functions. Above all, the planning process must be adaptable, flexible, and ongoing. It must also be an integral and continuous part of a public and community learning organization. It is the way the organization maintains coherence and relevance. It is not a one-time event involving only a few—it must be an ongoing organizational activity involving many. Because change is happening at such a rapid rate, the planners cannot afford to wait a year or more before getting feedback and making adjustments.

Involving the community and/or the organization in a meaningful way in the planning process requires the use of communication/information technologies. These technologies allow participation to happen in different ways and at different times. It will require the utilization of software that allows groups and individuals to participate, enables rapid response to proposals, summarizes and publishes input quickly, and provides for meaningful collaboration and consensus building on an ongoing basis.

Participants must be constantly vigilant and prepared for people who come to the process with claims that they know what to do and how to do it. Given the opportunity to plan for the future, most groups and organizations will use their experience and insight to re-create the past. Their attitudes and assumptions block their ability to see new realities. It is not uncommon to see the energies, resources, and creativity of the organization utilized to enhance practices that fall within the framework of an old paradigm.

In a knowledge-based organization everyone must be involved. Even if they can't participate directly, they need to know the framework in which the plan has been developed and have opportunity to input, validate, respond, align, and create system coherence around the information developed by those who participated in the planning process. In the knowledge-based society, the single basic unit of change is the individual and the structure of his or her thinking is the greatest enabler or blocker of change. Because of the emphasis on learning and knowledge for work and citizenship, this time might well become known as the *Age of the Mind*.

This planning process differs from its strategic counterpart because it encourages the development and application of learning systemwide. The responsibility for learning applies to both the component piece of the organization for which the individual or group is responsible as well as how that piece connects and impacts on the system it serves. It also promotes collaborative action around individual or group expertise. Terms of reference need to be developed that allow individuals and groups within the organization to take informed risks without penalty, try out ideas, confirm what works as well as what doesn't, and focus on the initiatives with the most potential in terms of the organization's overall mandate (see figure 19.1).

The diagram is a representation of the planning process described in the book. The center circle contains an expression about the core purpose or

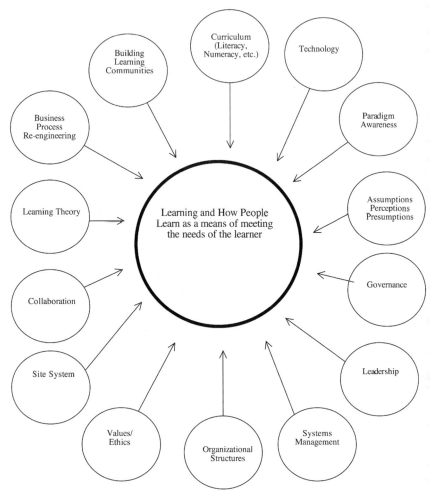

Figure 19.1. The pieces equal the whole

touchstone for the planning process. Around it are a number of components or pieces that represent the various areas of specialization that comprise a learning system. The circle, as opposed to a pyramid, suggests that all of the components have an equal, integrated and systemic role in making the core purpose happen.

It has been previously mentioned that participants in the planning process need to have the mindsets, skills, discipline, and insights to participate. With each component they will be asked to consider three questions in regard to creating a new system built around learning and how people learn and do it within the context of the Information Age. Those questions are as follows:

1. What past practices, processes, or organizational structures should be sustained?
2. What new practices, processes, or organizational structures need to be developed or acquired?
3. What practices, procedures, or organizational structures need to be eliminated or "unlearned"?

To prepare to participate in developing answers for these questions participants may wish to prepare by reflecting on the following questions:

1. How do we do this?
2. How do we work together to make this happen?
3. What skills do we need?
4. What tools do we need?
5. What resources do we need?
6. What mindset do we need?
7. Does this plan anticipate and include what needs to be done?
8. Are all parts of the system aligned in a coherent fashion and is what we are doing systemic and based on what we know about learning?
9. What are the organizational/cultural areas that need to be addressed?
10. What is the impact or implication if no change is made?
11. What are the political impacts of any suggested changes?
12. What or who has the most to lose by this change and how might they work against the proposed change or initiative?

Asking the right questions is one of the first steps in acquiring new learning and in developing or understanding new knowledge.

The knowledge-based planning model needs to establish a purpose that is bigger than individual interests and nurtures a belief that the planning process will make a difference. This requires the creation of an environment that encourages participation, involvement, and risk taking. Participants need to believe that what they plan will be implemented. Those who head organizations or those in governance must be prepared to support, resource, and implement the plan. Otherwise, credibility will be lost. That is part of creating the ethos or preconditions for planning.

It takes time to create a sense of what might be, the leadership skills to shift the organization in the desired direction, and the ability to harness the expertise,

creativity, and intellectual capital of those in the organization to develop and implement the plan.
    The planning process must be guided by a set of beliefs such as

- Systemic planning or knowledge-based planning provides the opportunity to make the *vision* come to life.
- The process will be inclusive, open, believable, relevant, and understandable. It will honor diversity of thought and opinion, and encourage and invite participation and contribution from a wide cross-section of participants in the organization.
- It will not add additional work to individuals or groups without a consideration of what tasks and activities are no longer necessary (i.e., the three questions around what we keep, what we acquire, and what we stop doing).
- It will transform issues, problems, and challenges into workable solutions.
- It will connect all aspects of the system or systems around a common perspective or focus (government, board, district, site, and partners).
- It will provide methods/tools/resources for implementation, inspire positive attitudes toward development, and change and include processes for assessing progress and retargeting where necessary.
- It will require a three- to five-year window, or even longer, for change to take place. Participants need to be prepared for this and develop mental models that will sustain their involvement over time. The constant is the process and the *inconstant* is the content. In the industrial age, the opposite is true.
- It will encourage informed risk taking.
- It will include a communication strategy that both sends and receives information on the status of the plan.
- It will bring together varied and sometimes competing interests in a way that serves the common good (focus on the learner).

    Participants must be aware that there is a downside to systemic thinking, especially if the planning process is trying to achieve a *oneness,* or trying to create a megasystem. In the case of banks, media conglomerates, and gas companies, this has led to reduced competition, reduced choice, and higher costs to the consumer. This should not be the goal for a learning system.
    Systems that converge and grow tend to do so with no consideration or reflection upon structural or operational weaknesses and points of vulnerability. In the era of global terrorism the drive for connectedness becomes a serious issue, especially in relation to hydro, telecommunication, financial, and transportation systems. A problem in one area can affect or threaten the survival of large segments of another. The October 2008 crises on Wall Street is a powerful example of what is wrong with this type of thinking and planning.

Therefore, the planning process must not only look at the creation of new form, function, and practice but must also formally assess the risk or vulnerability the system is now exposed to because of these new structures and relationships. Looking for what is a weakness or downside of any implementation must become part of our learning and thinking.

NOTE

1. Engraved on a church in Sussex, England (1730), SelfGrowth.com, www.selfgrowth.com/articles/Gray4.html.

Chapter Twenty

Creating a New Ethos

It is not too late. God's world has incredible healing powers. Within a single generation we could steer the earth towards our children's future. Let that generation start now, with God's help and blessing.[1]

Creating the practice, form, and function to guide individuals, organizations, institutions, and communities through the information age is an overwhelming task. Creating the environment or preconditions that foster their development may be even more difficult. It's not that it can't be done. It can. But creating an environment that constitutes a new ethos for societal action, thinking, and planning won't happen unless people understand why it needs to be done.

In the 1830s the preconditions that launched the industrial age in the United States included a high degree of literacy among its citizens, especially in the North, few centralized or bureaucratic rules, a spirit of entrepreneurship, and a belief and adherence to the organizing ideas presented by Descartes and Smith.

The preconditions for enabling the information age within our existing culture are similar but more complex. Literacy is still important but in an expanded form. These forms of literacy are foundations for the new cognitive infrastructure needed by citizens to successfully navigate the unchartered waters of the information age. Systems thinking and the ability to analyze and synthesize are also critical features of this mindset.

Certainly there is an urgency to move forward. The middle class is at risk and corporations are continuing to shift industrial age work and processes to other parts of the world. It is somewhat ironic that these corporations are helping to build the economy, and sometimes strategic capability, of other countries in order to make a profit but are doing so at the expense of the country that fostered their own growth and development.

Despite what the politicians say, the type of work that has sustained the middle class for many years and has been the foundation of a quality lifestyle is not likely to return. In some cases the natural resources have been depleted, manufacturing processes are outdated, and technology has replaced skill sets and work processes. Manual labor generates lower-end incomes. People in other parts of the world are willing to work longer and harder for much less than their North American counterparts. That is a truth that needs to be accepted. At the same time there needs to be some discussion about what actions can be taken to offset this trend. Letting people and their families fail is of little recommendation for any society.

The 2008 presidential primary process has generated some discussions about the issues and impact of outsourcing to other nations. There is seldom any discussion about the issues and impact of outsourcing within North America. It is clear that the social fabric of the American society is under a lot of strain. It is also clear that the eight-hundred-pound gorillas of race and gender are still in the room. Perhaps the progress that people felt has been achieved in these areas is not what it seems. There is still a lot of work to do as a society, both in the United States and Canada.

The primary process also has shown that there are great threats and concerns on the horizon. The projection that 28 million Americans will be on food stamps by the end of 2008, that other economies are bypassing those of the Western world, and that the gap between the haves and have nots is widening are significant benchmarks. Couple these with issues about failing infrastructure, the influence of special interests and lobbying, illegal immigration, ineffective government, record national debt, and failed schools, one cannot help but be concerned for the future.

Understanding the problem is the first step to finding resolution. The second step is understanding that new thinking, new skills, and new attitudes are needed to overcome these issues and circumstances. The new economy and the new work will be driven by the exploration of space, genetics, new forms of energy generation, environmental considerations, replacing aging infrastructure, and indeed, in the organizational and personal applications and practice associated with learning and how people learn. This new economy might also be driven by building a greater reliance on small businesses and less on the large corporations.

The emerging power and strength of China, Russia, and India generate a lot of discussion and speculation. It should be recognized, in that discussion, that these countries lack the compassion, the hope, and the generosity that, for all its faults, are contained in a democracy. They do not embrace the concept of a free citizenry with certain inalienable rights. Nor do they embrace the type of entrepreneurial spirit, generosity, and creative and critical thinking that democracies tend to promote.

The problems that face the Western democracies are common because the industrial age foundation upon which the economy was based is common. Therefore the solution to the problem also has some commonalities. That solution must be based on defining, understanding, and accepting that a new age is upon us and that we must change our practice, our thinking, and the way we organize, work, teach, and learn if we are to have any success in dealing with our issues. It is about creating a new ethos.

Do our mindsets about pieces support the continued separation, despite the rhetoric to the contrary, of society on an economic, racial, or ethnic basis? Would systems thinking help us resolve some of those issues and remove the walls and gates that impede our progress? And can we overcome the deep prejudice toward learning that exists within many parts of our society? These are points for discussion. If we continue to accept that only our brightest rise to the top and therefore there is only work and a quality lifestyle for a few, then we are indeed headed for serious trouble.

Nothing can or will happen quickly because people are still responding to the pieces that affect them most. They, for the most part, don't see the whole picture and therefore remain unaware of the danger. There is still too much belief that government is watching, knows what to do, cares, and will do the right thing. They don't and won't unless the people within the democracy assert their collective rights and responsibilities around new action.

It will take time and there needs to be interim solutions to help people out along the way. Certainly those out of work could be given jobs in rebuilding infrastructure, replanting forests, and restoring streams and lakes as well as inner cities. That could help them sustain a lifestyle and quality of life while dealing with the change agenda.

But how do you reengage a nation to be knowledgeable about the preconditions needed as well as the form or function of learning and learning systems? This is the beginning point or foundation upon which to base the renewal. The United States and Canada have faced challenges and threats before and have risen to the challenge. The ability is there, but is the will?

What is needed are individuals who have a place of respect and honor within the society to recognize the extent of the problem, its implications to the society, as well as the road to recovery. It would be the equivalent of the New Frontier speech given by President Kennedy, which would unite people around their commonalities in order to resolve their differences. But the people doing this must possess that most uncommon of skills of being able to take an idea this complex and speak about it in ways that are immediately clear and understood. He or she must have what they used to refer to as the *common touch*.

This will help citizens to commit to a future that would embrace the best of what is and what might be. To set the stage requires the presence and leadership of a Lincoln, a Roosevelt, a King, or a Jack or Bobby Kennedy. The challenge is nothing less than sustaining the democracy while transcending the industrial age; creating the societal points of equity, access, and opportunity; and developing new work, new skills, and a new economy around jobs that are only now beginning to be conceived.

NOTE

1. Pope John Paul II and Bartholomew I, Joint Declaration on Environment (2002), quoted at Sustainable Living.com, www.sustainableliving.com.au/profiles/celebrate/resources/quotes/?searchterm=Pope%20John%20Paul%20II.

Chapter Twenty-One

Imagine

Logic will get you from A to B. Imagination will take you everywhere.[1]

Imagine the following scenarios:

- A government, organized around information age thinking, with the political will and a belief in its citizens that would create a positive, embracing, and equitable future for everyone.
- The creation of systemic and open processes that would lead to the creation of learning systems based on the research about learning.
- A learning system that would in turn foster the re-creation of community as well as other organizations and institutions.
- A future driven by the common good and collective will of its citizens and not by the agendas of special or self-interest groups.
- A learning organization that embraces or includes in its practices the way we work and learn, in its form the way we are organized to work and learn, and in its function the purpose for why we work and learn.
- An all-encompassing vision statement cast within the context of twenty-first century thinking.
- A society that understands the differences between the two paradigms so that participants in the change process can participate in a meaningful way.
- A citizenry that acknowledges how the new organizing idea that drives the information age paradigm requires a different relationship between the site and the system—one that embraces learning, knowledge development, acquisition, and integration and formalizes both content and process management.
- A new model of governance that integrates systems with common purposes, makes the best use of resources, expects quality and excellence,

addresses lifelong learning needs for individuals and groups, and ensures that the needs of learners are valued first and foremost in an organization's activities.

- A knowledge-based planning model that facilitates that which is being imagined.
- New leadership models to create, support, implement, and sustain the needed change initiatives. This includes people who will manage the expertise or content that serves the core purpose of the organization and those who manage the processes to ensure that the *knowledge* informing the content is relevant, current, and available to all.
- Collaborative workplace environments based on an information age model of collaboration and leadership teams in order to maximize the organizational expertise available, to create innovations, to adapt quickly to change, and to create opportunities for members of the organization to build upon each other's knowledge and skill through the teaching/learning process.
- Decision makers who recognize the importance of learning to the creation of learning organizations and to the practice of knowledge building, knowledge sharing, knowledge acquisition, and knowledge construction.
- Business and engineering processes that help ensure that the resources and assets of the organization are used efficiently and applied effectively and fairly to achieve the overall purpose or goal of the organization and possibly to find funds on a systemic basis that could fund the reform.
- A re-created community with cognitive infrastructures that embrace learning as well as new mindsets, new thinking, new understandings, and new skills. Without a *co-changing* process, it would be difficult to create a new organization like a public learning system. The task is as simple and as difficult as changing the society in which we live—moving it from industrial age to information age content.
- A world that recognizes that technology is an important tool for change but that it is also a system and the environment in which much of the change must take place. Clearly, it plays a huge role in the management of the change process, the communication needs of a large number of participants for access to and distribution of information and knowledge, and the creation of new organizational function, form, and practice.
- The institutionalization of values and ethics based on learning and how people learn, within all aspects of the organization. Without them there can be no belief in the organizational vision, no trust in its leadership, and no support for creating, implementing, and sustaining change. It creates the organizational ether that fosters the hope and promise of what might be.
- The development of new assessment and evolution models to give us the *just-in-time* information needed to manage the change processes. It needs

to be systemic and it needs to involve the content and processes of the organization.

If it can be imagined—then it can be done. Doing so provides us with the opportunity to transcend our organizations, our communities, our society, and ourselves. Some will be overwhelmed at the prospect of doing this and will describe any notions about managing this type of change process as naive and wishful thinking. It will be a bridge too far. But one only has to envision the outcome of avoiding change to understand that, whether we like it or not, changes are coming. If we want to benefit from them as opposed to being destroyed by them, then we better find some way to change what we are doing. Do we wish to thrive or survive?

Our governments, our corporations, and our existing institutions are not providing either the leadership or launching the initiatives that will help our society make the shift it needs to. It is up to the people to collectively create in these leaders a sense of urgency and obligation to act for the collective good of all of us. Just imagine.

NOTE

1. Albert Einstein, quoted at ThinkExist.com, thinkexist.com/quotations/imagination/2.html.

Twenty-Two

Enabling a Future

As for the future, your task is not to foresee it, but to enable it.[1]

We have to stop seeing our public schools as separate and distinct pieces of society. Education cannot be viewed as a cost and not a benefit to the society. In fact the opposite is true. A society without the benefit of a quality education or learning system will suffer significant costs.

Thomas Jefferson understood the importance of a quality public education system to the economic, social, and political well-being of his country. He also understood that the societal framework was strengthened when all citizens were treated equally and given an opportunity to succeed based on their own hard work and initiative.

Increasingly, across North America, we see people's well-being or potential for success defined by the location in which they live and the access they have to services and programs. The walled cities within urban North America represent the haves while the have-nots can be within the inner cities and rural regions. Some have gates to keep people in and others have gates to keep people out.

In both Canada and the United States, there are public discussions by government about expanding private school, charter, and voucher systems as a means of deregulating education and creating more choice for parents. These notions may have validity in certain situations but not if they serve to widen the societal gap, in terms of access to quality service and opportunity, between those with wealth and those without.

Some of the standardized test data would indicate that there is a wide variance in achievement between and among schools. This division between those who did well and those who didn't was strongly represented along

153

racial lines with white students doing far better than African Americans and Hispanics. In Canada, similar distinctions exist between whites and First Nation or Aboriginal students. I suspect the reasons for these differences can be attributed to expectations for learning, resources, and quality of instruction.

Those communities with wealth and affluence are able to attract the more qualified teachers and tend to have more resources, better access to technology, and more volunteer or community support for their schools. Increasingly, we are seeing the same circumstances emerge between urban and rural achievement levels. Creating different levels of access to quality instruction and learning opportunities only serves to expand the division between the haves and the have nots. Yet these issues generally go unnoticed within our society. They exist within a disconnected environment in our communities in which there is little or no empathy for the welfare of others.

Maybe our society is a casualty of the interventions by centralized organizations. The intent of these interventions was well meaning in terms of empathy for specific groups, but the outcomes have created further inequities and divisions within the society. This is ironic in that our bureaucracies and their policies of social intervention may have created or nurtured that which they most abhor (i.e., inequity and social division). They have done this by centralizing control and weakening the community.

Governments and bureaucracies need to restore power to community so that communities have control over their own destiny. They need to work in partnership with communities, to create local capacity for change and strengthen the social fabric. They can address those issues that need to be handled systemically by collaboratively setting the *what* of community and empowering people within communities to create and lead the *how* of change.

Having a quality public learning system is a way of addressing the social, economic, and political divisiveness and discord found in our society. It is a reform that must take place if our children and grandchildren are to have any hope and, indeed, if the society is to have any hope. It is not a reform that can take place in pieces, nor can it be done by an individual organization.

It is a reform that must take place within the context of community. It may be a symbiotic event in that the reform of public education also implies the reconstruction or reinvention of community. We must provide opportunities for all people to learn and contribute in a meaningful way and support for those who are unable to participate.

Government is not asking the right questions about what needs to change. It lacks the understanding and the political will to begin an open and honest dialogue with citizens about what needs to happen. It does not share information or resources in a way that is mutually beneficial to all concerned. Its political and bureaucratic leaders enshrine the notion of power and influence—a power and influence that is often used to further special agendas that have nothing to do with the common good. We should be wary of anyone who thinks that government can be reformed by changing expectations or policy. It can't and won't.

Communities need to become reenfranchised so that they regain the capacity to address their needs. Otherwise the change we need will not happen. Governments need to be part of the process. They need to collaboratively set the terms of reference for what needs to be accomplished and provide the resources, opportunity, and support for communities depending on individual circumstances.

Even more important to this reform concept is the need for broad and inclusive conversations about the need for change. These conversations should provide a consideration of what each individual group or organization can contribute in resources or expertise to the process. This includes a commitment to the concept of community and to its values and beliefs. Those who represent government and government bureaucracies in local communities will be challenged to work and think in ways that are opposite to current practice.

The crisis around the Bill Clinton presidency and the discussion about the loss of respect for the presidency sparked a lot of discussion about the need for heroes. A commentator on one news program reflected that it was difficult today for any one person to assume hero status, in any area of society, because of the persistent intrusion of communication/information technologies into the private lives of citizens.

In a speech to the Kennedy School of Government, Mario Cuomo, the former governor of New York, said that "the ground is too hard for heroes to grow."[2] In other words, the circumstances of present society make it difficult for a hero to emerge within our midst. If that is the case, then maybe what we need to do is focus on heroic ideals to which all of us can aspire. True heroes will rise from those aspirations.

One has only to watch Frank Capra's 1939 movie *Mr. Smith Goes to Washington*, starring Jimmy Stewart, to understand that comment. The story is built around an individual's idea of heroic ideals, of loving your neighbor and "looking out for the other fella." It is the spirit that our communities need to reinstill into community life. These attitudes create the kind of community that will embrace, explore, and implement the changes needed. It will also help them build around the positive notions of communities that learn, as well as build and share knowledge collaboratively.

Society has always needed to strive to meet heroic ideals more than they needed heroes. Heroes are a manifestation of what we think we are, while heroic ideals are a manifestation of what we might be. The up-to-the-minute media coverage that permeates our daily lives reminds us that no one is perfect. The media is very quick to report, as we are to listen, about the personal failures of those trying to assume or sustain leadership roles within our society.

We need to grow and mature as a society so that we are not surprised by human behavior. We know that perfect beings can't and don't exist, and we need to recognize that those who strive to attain and accomplish that which is most good, or worthy, display heroic behavior.

The issues in front of us are challenging, but they are achievable. The ideals may be of heroic proportion but the significance of not trying to accomplish the task sets the stage for a tragedy beyond our imagination. It is not a given that the ideals of democracy and the concept of equity of opportunity and participation for all citizens are enshrined in the thinking of political powerbrokers. Consequently, it is imperative that they are enshrined in the hearts and minds of citizens. It is up to us to be vigilant, to be informed, to be knowledgeable, and to participate.

As citizens, we must be prepared to exercise our rights and privileges, especially in the service of learning, because learning is the key to being vigilant, competent, and informed. Relevant learning systems strongly connected to the social, economic, and political well-being of our communities is the place to begin the shaping and structuring of the new paradigm. If only a few people understand the new rules, and if affluence is the key to quality education and participation in our society, then we will have placed in danger the very notion of our individual and collective freedom.

China and India, perhaps the two fastest-growing economies in the world, have a different reality. Their decision makers face virtually no opposition to their thinking and they are unencumbered by the form, function, and practice of industrial age culture. They are open to new ideas and innovations that pertain to the information age society: ideas and innovations that will give them an economic advantage over their rivals.

We on the other hand are like the football, baseball, or hockey team that created a successful dynasty but are closed to real change because they don't want to interfere with the structures that brought them success. We need the truth to drive us to a new reality. But we have tunnel vision where the future is concerned—believing that what we have done to get us to this point will continue to sustain us.

This is dangerous thinking for a sports team but even more dangerous for a society. Falling from grace and ending up on the bottom of your division is usually a motivator for renewal, recovery, and success. For a society, the implications are far more severe, although history teaches us that we generally have to face a catastrophe before we become united and respond to the threat and before we can *get back into the game.*

Our preschool, public school, college, university, and workplace training infrastructures are a huge asset to our society, but only if they can be reformed to serve the purpose of educating us for new learning. This requires cooperation and an individual, organizational, and political will, similar to what was seen during World War II. As difficult as it may be, the process of unlearning our past and inventing our future is the beginning point of that process. It is the way to sustain a way of life and a set of beliefs.

If the West is in a decline then maybe this is the way to renew and to reestablish ourselves. As David McCullough, the Pulitzer Prize–winning biographer said, "We are living now in an era of momentous change, of huge transitions, in all aspects of life here, nationwide, worldwide and this creates great pressures and tensions. But history shows that times of change are the times when we are most likely to learn."[3]

Will we experience another *Age of Darkness* as we shift from one paradigm to another, or will it be a Renaissance that celebrates learning and the dignity of the human spirit? If some of the fundamentalists, both Christian and Islamic, were to have their way we would move to something that is the equivalent of the Dark Ages, because of their notions about the supremacy of the past. If we continue to go where we are headed, we will see many examples that exemplify the worst of human nature. This will not be new because history shows us that it has all been done before.

But if we are wise and if we are thoughtful, then maybe, just maybe, we could do the best things that we could imagine. This would be something new. History shows that doing what is best for all of us when faced with adversity, but before tragedy, has seldom been a societal focus. But just perhaps, in a time that honors knowledge and learning, we may collectively gain the wisdom to do just that.

The future is not a given and it is not predestined. We do not have to be at the whim and mercy of individuals or special interest groups that would readily sacrifice what we hold most dear in exchange for their personal gain. Neither do we need to become enslaved to systemized ignorance. By becoming better informed and better skilled at information age citizenship, we embrace the potential to invent the future we need and not accept the one that will be bestowed upon us because of indifference, ignorance, and self-interest.

"There is in the worst of fortune the best of chances for a happy change."[4]

NOTES

1. Antoine de Saint-Exupery, quoted at Innovation Watch, www.innovation-watch.com/future.htm.

2. Dara Horn, "A Governor Cries in the ARCO Forum," *Harvard Crimson*, February 25, 1999, www.thecrimson.com/article.aspx?ref=95831.

3. Dave Weich, "Connecting with David McCullough," Powells.com, May 25, 2005, www.powells.com/authors/mccullough.html.

4. Euripides, QuoteWorld.org, www.quoteworld.org/quotes/4629.

Select Bibliography

Brands, H. W. *The First American: The Life and Times of Benjamin Franklin.* New York: Anchor Books, 2000.

Boorstein, Daniel J. *The Discoverers: A History of Man's Search to Know His World and Himself.* New York: Random House, First Vintage Book Edition, 1985.

Burke, James. "Inventors and Inventions, Accidents plus Luck: The Sum of Innovation Is Greater Than Its Parts." *Time Magazine,* December 4, 2000. www.time.com/time/asia/magazine/2000/1204/inventions.html.

Canadian Council on Learning. "The State of Learning in Canada: No Time for Complacency," *Report on Learning in Canada 2007* (Ottawa: 2007). www.ccl-cca.ca/NR/rdonlyres/5ECAA2E9-D5E4-43B9-94E4-84D6D31BC5BC/0/NewSOLR_Report.pdf

Davidow, William H., and Michael S. Malone. *The Virtual Corporation.* New York: Collins Publishers, 1992.

Drucker, Peter F. *Post-Capitalist Society.* New York: HarperCollins, 1993.

Enriquez, Juan. *As the Future Catches You.* New York: Crown Business, 2000.

Feller, Ben. "Governors Work to Improve H.S. Education." *Associated Press,* February 26, 2005. www.democraticunderground.com/discuss/duboard.php?az=view_all&address=102x1268452.

Fishman, Ted C. "The Forum—Betting on China." *USA Today,* February 17, 2005, 11a.

Friedman, Thomas L. "It's a Flat World After All." *New York Times,* April 3, 2005. www.nytimes.com/2005/04/03/magazine/03DOMINANCE.html?_r=1&oref=slogin&pagewanted=print&position=.

Friedman, Thomas L. *The World Is Flat: A Brief History of the Twenty-First Century.* New York: Farrar, Straus and Giroux, 2005.

Hammer, Michael, and James Champy. *Reengineering the Corporation.* New York: HarperCollins, 1994.

Hayward, Steven F. *Churchill on Leadership.* Rocklin, CA: Prima Publishing, 1997.

Johnston, Peter. "The Media Mix." *USA Today,* February 14, 2005. www.usatoday.com/life/columnist/mediamix/2005-02-14-media-mix_x.htm.

McClaren, Milton. "EECO Week 3. Design for Learning. The Challenges and Opportunities of Human Diversity in the Design of Learning Environments." Course notes, Royal Roads University, Victoria, B.C., 2007.

McCullough, David. *1776.* New York: Simon & Schuster, 2005.

McCullough, David. *Truman.* New York: Simon & Schuster, 1993.

McLuhan, Marshall. *Understanding Media: The Extensions of Man.* New York: McGraw-Hill, 1964.

McLuhan, Marshall, and Quentin Fiore. *The Medium Is the Massage.* New York: Bantam Books, 1967.

National Academy of Sciences, M. Suzanne Donovan, John D. Bransford, and James W. Pellegrino, eds., Summary of *How People Learn: Bridging Research and Practice.* Washington, D.C.: National Academy Press, 1999. www.nap.edu/html/howpeople2/notice.html.

Phillips, Donald T. *Lincoln on Leadership: Executive Strategies for Tough Times.* New York: Warner Books, 1993.

ProLiteracy America. "U.S. Adult Literacy Programs: Making a Difference." U.S. Programs Division of ProLiteracy Worldwide, March 2003. www.proliteracy.org/downloads/LitOutPDF.pdf.

Schmidt, Sarah. "Declining Skills Force University to Offer More Remedial Classes." *Vancouver Sun,* March 8, 2005, 7A.

Smith, Jean Edward. *Grant.* New York: Simon & Schuster, 2001.

Stein, Ben. "In Class Warfare, Guess Which Class Is Winning." *New York Times,* November 26, 2006. www.nytimes.com/2006/11/26/business/yourmoney/26every.html?ex=1322197200&en=0cf857b8cb918674&ei=5088&partner=rssnyt&emc=rss.

Surgenor, Everette. *Pioneering the Mindscape: Designing Learning Systems for the Information Age.* Vancouver: EduServe, 1992.

Toffler, Alvin. *The Third Wave.* New York: Morrow, 1980.

Ward, Doug. "The Daily Special—Blogging: The New Soapbox." *Vancouver Sun,* February 19, 2005, B2/B3.

About the Author

Everette Surgenor has worked in the past few years with some small, rural, resource-dependent communities in the Kootenay region of British Columbia whose future is challenged by rapidly changing economic and social variables. He retired from public education in 2003 after thirty years of service to learners in a variety of assignments at the classroom, school, district, and regional levels. He was appointed by the Minister of Education for the Province to serve on a Rural Task Force in 2003 and was recognized by the Province of British Columbia in 2005 for his work with technology and network building.